FABULOUS FINISHES
for Your Home
STEP BY STEP

Fabulous
Finishes
for Your Home
STEP BY STEP

KARL-HEINZ MESCHBACH

NORTH LIGHT BOOKS
CINCINNATI, OHIO

A NOTE ABOUT SAFETY

Due to toxicity concerns, most art material manufacturers have begun labeling their products with proper health warnings or nontoxic seals. It is always important to read a manufacturer's label thoroughly when using a product for the first time. Follow any warnings about not using the product when pregnant or contemplating pregnancy; about keeping it out of the reach of children; and about mixing incompatible products. Always work in a well-ventilated room when using products with fumes.

The information in this book is presented in good faith, but no warranty is given, nor results guaranteed, nor is freedom from any patent to be inferred. Since we have no control over physical conditions surrounding the application of products, techniques and information contained herein, the author and publisher disclaim any liability for results.

Fabulous Finishes for Your Home Step by Step. Copyright © 1999 by Karl-Heinz Meschbach. Manufactured in China. All rights reserved. No part of this book may be reproduced in any form or by any electronic or mechanical means including information storage and retrieval systems without permission in writing from the publisher, except by a reviewer, who may quote brief passages in a review. Published by North Light Books, an imprint of F&W Publications, Inc., 1507 Dana Avenue, Cincinnati, Ohio 45207. (800) 289-0963. First edition.

Other fine North Light Books are available from your local bookstore, art supply store or direct from the publisher.

03 02 01 00 99   5 4 3 2 1

Library of Congress Cataloging-in-Publication Data

Meschbach, Karl-Heinz
   Fabulous finishes for your home step by step / Karl-Heinz Meschbach.
      p.   cm.
   ISBN 0-89134-921-9
   1. House painting. 2. Decoration and ornament. 3. Finishes and finishing. I. Title.
TT323.M46   1999
698′.14—dc21
                                                         99-14290
                                                              CIP

Editor: Roseann Biederman
Production editors: Amy J. Wolgemuth and Nicole R. Klungle
Designer: Sandy Conopeotis Kent
Cover designer: Brian Roeth
Production coordinator: Erin Boggs
Photo credits: Greg Albert, Diane Griffin, Karl-Heinz Meschbach

ABOUT THE AUTHOR

At age 14, Karl-Heinz Meschbach began formal training at the *Berufsschule für Maler* in Berlin, specializing in decorative painting. He studied under Masters Rocke and Herrmann in the European Guild tradition and won numerous commendations and awards, including second place in a national competition. In 1960 he was awarded the prestigious Berlin City and Guild Certification as a decorative painter.

Karl-Heinz worked as a mural painter in East Germany and Austria until his escape to West Germany in 1961. After one year in Cologne, he emigrated to the United States, settled in Chicago and joined the U.S. Army.

Karl-Heinz held his first solo exhibition in 1965 while stationed in Schwabach, West Germany. After active service he returned to Chicago and worked as a paper hanger, house painter, muralist and fine artist. During this period, he published or exhibited over 100 pen-and-ink drawings.

In 1973 Karl-Heinz changed his emphasis to oil painting and exhibited his work in major Illinois universities and galleries, including the Art Institute of Chicago. He moved to northern Minnesota in 1982 to establish a homestead and find a more creative environment. Four years later, he relocated to Circle Pines, Minnesota. Although he now lives in Dushore, Pennsylvania, Karl-Heinz maintains a studio in Circle Pines with emphasis on the application of fine art in decorative painting and design. He also works with da Vinci, a traditional German brush maker, expanding their line of fine decorative painting brushes. These exceptional brushes as well as other top-quality tools are marketed under the name "The Faux Meister."

Member of:

♦ The Ancient and Honorable Guild of Painters
♦ The Society of Decorative Painters
♦ The British Association of Decorative and Folk Arts
Honorable Member:
♦ Decorative Artists of Argentina

Dedication

In fond memory of Gerry Albrecht, VGM, a fine artist and friend.

Acknowledgments

Thanks to the editors and staff of North Light Books and
to my mother, Gertrud, who made it all possible.

TABLE *of* CONTENTS

Part 1
EASY FAUX FINISH TECHNIQUES
18

Part 2
ECLECTIC FAUX FINISH TECHNIQUES
54

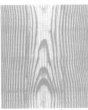

Part 3
ELEGANT FAUX FINISH TECHNIQUES
86

Marbling and Graining in Folk Art:

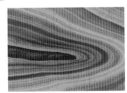

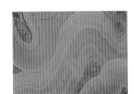

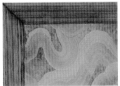

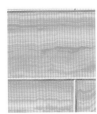

*D*ecorative painting has been used for centuries in interior and exterior decoration by architects and designers, as well as by artists and crafters of the smaller wooden, metal and ceramic objects that make our lives more interesting and enjoyable.

This book is concerned with the techniques often, and to a degree erroneously, called faux (pronounced *foe*) finishes. This term is of French derivation and loosely translated means "false," or "looking like or imitating something else." Although many of the techniques covered in this book may be used in replicating marble, stone, wood or leather, these same techniques may also be used to create fantasy finishes that do not replicate the appearance of natural materials. So the term *faux finish* is loosely used to refer to all of these applications. This book does not try to change the way most painters think of this term, but it does try to promote better communication between you (the painter) and those who are the fortunate recipients of the fruits of your labor.

This book uses terms most descriptive of the specific techniques being discussed, thereby avoiding the tendency to lump all of the techniques together. For example, the term *marbling* is used to describe the process of rendering an illusion of real marble and not to describe a simple glazing or ragging technique. *Faux* is used whenever a technique is used to imitate a product of nature.

As a matter of clarification, the issue of ethnicity needs to be addressed. Historically, ethnic painting—such as Norwegian rosemaling, German bauernmalerei, Swedish dålmalning and Russian zhostova—has been a peasant's specific use of the decorative painting techniques that have been used by professional craftspeople throughout the civilized world for centuries. Lately, *French painting* has been used as a catch-all for finishing techniques. In reality, although French peasants did copy the professionals as did peasants of other countries, they did not invent faux finish techniques as implied by the overused term *French painting*. As discussed above, the word *faux* has come to be used in ways other than its actual meaning. Perhaps the association with the French has come about because *faux* is a French word. Since this book is written in English, however, English terms will be used whenever possible.

Samples of woodgraining from Egypt have survived millennia, and the Italians have used finishing techniques in murals for centuries. The paintings of Pompeii are some of the earliest examples of professional decorative painting and are still some of the most colorful and beautifully rendered to date. Credit also needs to be given to craftsmen such as John Taylor, Thomas Kershaw and Cornelius Hebing, who worked during the mid-nineteenth century and set standards that are seldom equaled today. Thus, decorative painting in general and finishing techniques in specific are multicultural phenomena and not exclusively French. References to specific cultural or ethnic decoration should, therefore, be referred to as *peasant painting*.

In learning about decorative finishing techniques, we must build on what was done in the past. It is important to know that one reason decorative painting of recent centuries has endured for us to enjoy today is due to the development of oil paints. Prior to these paints, pigments and painting tools were crude and impermanent. After their development, it was possible to truly fool the eye with paint—for example, when using a badger hair brush to soften an oil glaze, as done in marbling and woodgraining. No significant changes or improvements in the manufacturing of these specialty tools have been necessary since the mid-nineteenth century. Brushes are still made of natural hair and bristle by the skilled hands of the certified members and masters of the brush makers guild. Even when working with synthetic paints (acrylics), natural hair brushes are the only prudent choice. In most endeavors, they far outperform those manufactured with man-made fibers, especially when imitating nature.

Certain tools and supplies are common to all fundamental faux painting techniques. Supplies unique to a particular technique are provided with the instructions for that technique, and most of these materials can be found in any good paint supply store.

Until the 1850s, most paints were made by the individual guild painter or artist, as well as by crafters, hobbyists and peasant painters. The guild artist used his master's secrets and, over time, developed unique concoctions suited for a specific purpose or environmental condition. Included were paints such as various malt-, milk-, oil-, egg-, plant extract-, hide-, bone-, lime-, gypsum- and silicate-based products. We can suspect that virtually everything was tried. Those mentioned were and still are excellent painting materials not only for the so-called faux finisher.

Paint and brush manufacturing by the guilds began in the early fourteenth century. However, for the past 150 years, the production of paints has shifted from the professional manufacturer or individual painter and artist to the factory chemist and industrial laborer. The only innovations have been latex paint, made from the milk of rubber trees, and its synthetic cousin, acrylic, as well as all poly-based paints.

Although the *open time*, or time a material can be molded or manipulated, is rather short for acrylics, they compare well with most of the earlier paints. Some of the lower hobby- or student-grade products are dubious and rarely fulfill their promises—the finished product may prove to be of little value. The use of better-grade artist-quality, hobby and house-painting tools and materials is recommended. This is not to say that you must buy solely according to the price tag. Listen, test and learn to discern the differences, and trust with caution. Remember, your friendly professional paint salesperson may have sold shoes until the day before and it is unlikely that he will admit this to you.

When you complete a project and are ready to dispose of your paints, keep in mind that paints, even those that are water-soluble, are not food products. Acrylic paints are polymer-based, liquid-plastic materials. Some contain additives such as glycol, antifreeze and formaldehyde to slow deterioration. Disposing of such materials into our most precious resource, drinking water, should be avoided. Recycling methods for synthetic paints are now being introduced in Europe.

SUPPLIES AND PRODUCTS
Faux finishing supplies: acrylic paints, extender, glazing medium and denatured alcohol.

When using natural and artificial paints, including latex and acrylics, some allergic reactions may result. Nausea and headaches are two typical symptoms, as well as skin irritation and rashes. For more information regarding any health and safety concerns and the use of artists' materials, consult *Artists Beware*, by Michael McCann. **Note: *Always read the instructions and warnings on the products you use.***

Paints

Latex and acrylics

These are water-based products. Keep in mind that the term *latex* is used figuratively by many paint manufacturers. The name often appears on the can but upon reading the label, no latex or rubber products can be found in the product. For our purposes, the terms *latex* and *acrylic* are used to refer to the same product. Acrylic is, in a sense, synthetic latex. Good-quality interior paints are an excellent choice for most projects. There are, of course, other time-tested paints, such as casein, watercolor and vinegar, but we will focus on acrylics.

Sheen

Paints come in a variety of sheens, that is, the reflective quality of the surface when dry. And there is no consistently used word to describe the sheen of a paint. What may be *semigloss* to one manufacturer is *satin* or *eggshell* to another, or *high gloss* to yet another. Some companies may also use the term *luster* instead of *sheen*. Generally, *flat* is the lowest sheen, having little or no sheen, and then eggshell, satin, semigloss and high gloss.

Many paint stores have samples of what sheen a paint will take on when dry. It is best to check these samples first, then select your paint accordingly. The sheen required will vary with each painting technique. The higher the sheen, the easier the glaze lifts off or is manipulated on the surface. A high-gloss surface must be sanded to dull the surface before a glaze is applied. This will create a surface to which glazes can adhere. To do this, use a very fine sandpaper such as 220 grit, or, even better, use wet/dry sand with a silicon carbide paper of the same fine grit.

Color

This book does not discuss specific colors when presenting the fundamental techniques. The particular hue you choose will be dictated by your needs. The paint may be premixed at the store and altered by adding colorants purchased at the paint store. Universal colorants are pigments suspended in detergent or glycol so that they may be used in either oil- or water-based products. They are the colors used in paint store machines, but can also be purchased in containers of various sizes.

Nonstandardized colors are created by adding colorants to paint. However, many paint stores provide a chart with color names and numbers assembled by the Color Guild Associates. Keep in mind that an effect achieved by painting a dark color over a light color will be different if the values are reversed. Experimenting with small quantities on practice boards is the best way to decide which paints to use.

Varnishes and Shellacs

Varnishes such as Spar varnish are unstable by nature and design. They work best for exterior use, expanding and contracting with extreme changes in moisture and temperature conditions. High-gloss varnish is smooth and tough. Lower sheen varnish is essentially high-gloss varnish dulled by the addition of wax or wax substitutes. The lower the sheen of the varnish, the softer, less durable and more porous it becomes.

For the most part, shellacs are fast-drying sealants with hard finishes and are available in varying weights. The old-fashioned orange shellac (also called amber shellac) has limited use for our purposes. Clear shellac may be used as a fixative or sealant over a finish but, because contact with moisture may discolor the surface, it must eventually be covered with a varnish. Pigmented or white shellac is an excellent stain eliminator that will cover magic marker and water damage. To protect most interior work done in acrylic paints and glazes, use acrylic sealants and varnishes. Two coats are necessary in most cases. And remember to check the expiration date. If an outdated product is used, there may be problems with drying time.

Sanding

I use grits from 120–400 for most purposes. Obviously, you would not use a rough paper on gypsum drywall. The finer or more fragile the surface, the finer the paper you'll need to use. Raw wood or a rough-grained, recently primed surface will need a rougher paper.

Silicon carbide sandpaper is a medium or fine paper that is used with water. You may use it dry, but water acts as a buffer, resulting in a very finely sanded surface.

A sanding sponge is a useful tool

catalog; or you may already have them around your house.

When using synthetic materials, you should use artificial fiber brushes. However, you may find that natural hair and bristle, or a combination of both, perform better and last longer. In either case, it is not necessary to use the best-quality tools for simple tasks, but don't be tempted to use a cheap brush for *any* painting purpose. It will frustrate even a menial effort, but even more so one that requires a measure of quality and care.

Be cautious and educated in the subject of any purchase; for instance, some companies apply traditional names of tools to their modern versions. One good modern example is the sword striper, which is a pinstriping brush that many prefer over the traditional goose feather for veining faux marble. Such brushes range in size from nos. 2/0 to 5 with handles 1½ to 2 inches long and have Blue or Kasan squirrel hairs arranged in a flat ferrule to look like the blade of a sword. On one side the hairs are about ¾ of an inch long and on the other side they are about 2 inches long. This creates a brush that has a full body to hold a great amount of paint, yet has a very fine and delicate tip. Another traditional brush has longer hairs in the center; it is called a dagger striper due to its shape. But be cautious of the modern version, which is only about a ½-inch long from ferrule to tip, and thus a bit short. Also, the modern dagger stripers are swordlike in shape, curved from the hilt to a point on one side, which is incorrect. This brush spells double trouble: it's too short and has the wrong shape.

Most tools have distinct quality differences. The reasons why vary

that is easy to hold and adapts to the contours of any surface, making it especially helpful for working on furniture or moldings. Sanding blocks are useful only for very flat surfaces.

Avoid using so-called liquid "sandpaper in a can." These sanding substitutes may claim that, by simply brushing them on, the magic of science will do the job for you. Wrong! Besides, by doing the sanding yourself, you will know what you have to work with and enter into the classic love-hate relationship with a piece of wood. If you both survive, it will be worth the effort.

Brushes and Tools

Finer, realistic wood and marble imitations require, besides a certain amount of skill and experience, a few special tools of the trade. Some of these may look unusual or even bizarre to the novice, as well as to the painter who has not been introduced to faux finishing. Some of these tools are rather costly. For example, a good 3-inch pure badger softener costs between $85 and $200, and a 2½-inch

Calcutta bristle flogger ranges from $35 to $55. However, these are the extremes. Other brushes, such as various mottlers, range from $2.50 to $35 depending on the type, size and hair.

Fortunately, the most expensive of these tools can last one to two generations if—and this cannot be stressed enough—they are properly cared for. This is crucial to their proper performance as well as prudent for obvious economic reasons. Traditional wisdom proves that only the correct use of a pure plant-based curd soap will be adequate for this task. Brush soap, which is usually made of nut oils, not only cleans synthetic and natural hairs and bristles, it also restores natural oils to the brush head, thus returning the hair or bristle to its original smoothness, elasticity and spring.

This book purposely refrains from using most specialized tools usually associated with faux finishing. The brushes used in the projects are of good or reasonable quality. You can find them, as well as the other materials, in any artist, hobby or house paint supply store; or you can buy some of them through an appropriate

from a manufacturer that may care less about the tools it produces and thus produces look-alikes, or a brush maker who has an occasional bad day and makes an inferior-quality brush. Differences can also be discerned by logical investigation, for example, a rocker or heartgrainer made of solid rubber generally performs better and lasts longer than one made of plastic. Rubber "gives" more and thus makes better contact with the work surface. So inspect, investigate, buy smart and then take good care of your investments.

Sponges

While all sponges may be created equal, their textures are quite individual. The best sponges for our purposes are nicely rounded on at least one side. Their texture on that side should be even and can be fine to coarse. The texture you will produce is largely determined by the texture

of the sponge, so choose a sponge to fill your requirements and tastes. A medium coarse texture is the most accepted and versatile choice.

It will take a few test applications to develop a sense of what works best, so until you are sure of getting what you want simply by looking at a dry sponge, test its pattern on a practice board. A sponge that gives you an ugly texture should be discarded or used to wash the car. Sponges to avoid include flat sponges (so called "elephant's ears"); sponges that are tattered, without texture or rather hard; and most sea grass sponges, which have lengthy tentacles.

Rags

Natural cotton fibers work best since they absorb well. You do not need to purchase new bedsheets for your next ragging job as one of my students did. Instead, recycle old ones or

purchase select clean box lots at your local paint outlet. But be sure to look at them first—some crafty stores include poor-quality rags that are useless for our purposes. The best choice is brand-new remnant stock from T-shirt or bedding factories.

Masking Tape and Drop Cloths

Of course, you need to protect areas that are not to be painted. Do this by taping, covering and carefully cutting in. Cutting in is the process in which a sharp line is created by painting along the edge of tape, or when corners and bases are brushed in where rollers cannot reach. It requires practice and good-quality tools. Angular brushes may prove to be the easiest to get used to, however, flat, oval and round brushes will perform with equal efficiency. For taping, try 3M's Longmask tape. Developed primarily for exterior work, it seals well without releasing glue when removed. Furniture is best covered with plastic. For covering floors, I prefer using good-quality drop cloths and runners. Paper, old sheets or curtains may also be used, but avoid using plastic on floors—it is not only dangerous, but can become self-defeating.

General cleanup requires only soap and warm water. Unwanted acrylic paint that has dried on surfaces other than acrylic can be dissolved with denatured or rubbing alcohol. Be aware that some manufacturers "stretch" their products by adding water.

Gloves

Wear sensible clothing and protect your hands, especially when you will

have excessive direct contact with paints. If you are allergic to latex gloves (and, therefore, most likely to latex paints), wear rubber gloves and consider using alternative materials. Lotions, Vaseline and liquid glove-type products may be worth considering, but use them with discretion.

Paint Tray

When decorating large areas, use a paint tray, which provides a sort of workstation. The paint is kept in the deep part of the slanted tray, and the tools on the higher part.

Tack Cloth

A tack cloth is an indispensable tool when preparing a surface where finer sanding between coats is necessary. Essentially, this is a cheesecloth that has been made sticky with a combination of linseed oil, varnish and waxes. I use commercial brands, but any brand will do. They all effectively remove the finest dust particles from a surface.

Material Lists

There are tools and materials common to all painting projects. It is sensible to always have a rag on hand, as well as water for cleaning up a spill, rinsing out a sponge or brush or slightly thinning a paint or glaze. You will also need an artist's or house-painter's paintbrush and, for larger projects, a roller to apply a layer of glaze. And finally, you'll need the necessary items for preparing a surface to be painted and for protecting yourself and the areas around you from unwanted paint.

The preceding list of materials is very basic because you should always read and understand the instructions prior to beginning any project. In fact, practice the technique first instead of holding the instructions in one hand, a brush in the other and finding halfway through the process that you need an item you don't have. Also, don't scramble to purchase specialty tools such as a softener, flogger, mottler and overgrainer. While these tools may enhance your efforts, they are not necessary. If, on the other hand, you own or have access to these brushes, then use them.

*I*n any undertaking, you must make sure you have a good foundation. Remember— the most important steps in painting are the preparation and the finish. Proper surface preparation ensures good adhesion of your faux painting and the finish protects your hard-won decoration. It is important to prepare the surface according to the best professional standards, but the actual process will vary according to the condition and type of surface.

New Interior Walls

New plasterboard, gypsum wallboard or drywall (also known by the brand name Sheetrock) must be properly prepared before wielding a paint-brush. The joints must first be taped, patched and sanded. If you need more information on this procedure, contact your local hardware or lumber store. Then prime the walls with a polymer vinyl acetate (PVA) primer, which is a latex-based primer that ensures adhesion and prevents graying or bleeding of the board's paper cover and filler. This should be followed with one or two applications of the base coat.

Old Interior Walls

Common sense is your best ally when working with old walls. You need to determine what will allow the best and most permanent application of the glazes. The surface should be sound. If necessary, wash it with a nonphosphorus soap, patch it as needed and then sand. Two dependable products for patching are Dura-bond for larger areas and Syncaloid's spackle for smaller holes and nicks. Spot prime these areas once or, better yet, twice with PVA or a suitable acrylic/latex paint. Avoid using quick-drying products such as lacquer- or shellac-based primers, except when isolating water stains and marker and pen marks, since they may not properly adhere to the surface.

Now apply the undercoat. Use a brush or low-nap roller for a smooth base and good coverage. To avoid the "fuzzies" from the roller sleeve, use a previously used and washed sleeve or a good-quality sponge roller sleeve with at least one rounded edge such as the Master-Painter's Moltoprene. Remember that a good tool will pay for itself in a superior end result as well as be more satisfying to use while painting.

Finally, check your work. Be critical. If necessary, redo it. A good base will pay off in the final product.

Interior Woodwork

Wood breathes by expanding and contracting with changes in temperature and humidity. Since wood is vulnerable, good adhesion is the best guarantee for a lasting finish and it begins with the first coat of paint— the primer. Opaque coverage is not necessary since the purpose of a primer on raw wood is to penetrate the surface—the deeper, the better. This penetration is paramount to insure adhesion of the first coat of paint. Then, by sanding and using proper paints on clean surfaces (free of wax, oil, and dirt), you insure that these paints will properly adhere to each previous finish.

Use a good-quality oil- or alkyd-based primer. Using water-based paints to prime is a new and, in my opinion, questionable practice. For deeper penetration, add about a shot glass each of boiled linseed and paint thinner to a quart of primer. To speed the drying process, add half of a shot glass of Japan drier to the quart. Again, avoid the use of nonpenetrating, shellac- or alcohol-based, quick-dry products. I have seen them fail miserably.

Sand and dust off the wood surface and fill in any holes with spackle or other wood filler. Then sand again. Dust off the surface, tack it with a tack cloth and prime the surface again. Use the primer product

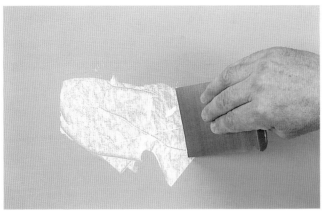

SPACKLING
Cover walls and ceiling with several applications of spackling compound or plaster patch to correct holes and irregularities.

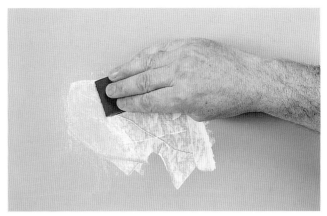

SANDING
Sand walls and ceilings to smooth bumps and layers of spackling compound or plaster patch. The finer (or more fragile) the surface, the finer the sanding paper.

unadulterated—thin it only enough to make the product easier to apply. If the primer is the base coat, you may tint it and any subsequent coats. If complete coverage is necessary, prime, sand and tack again. You should now have a well-covered, smooth surface.

If your needs call for a coat of a particular sheen of paint, it should be applied at this time. If you are using a high-gloss coating, it should be sanded before the glaze is applied. The surface should be smooth, not glossy.

Old Prepainted Interior Wood

Working on an old painted wood surface will always requires a judgment call. No one likes to strip woodwork or furniture, but that may be necessary to ensure the best possible finish. Be careful not to be lured into employing a company to dip or immerse the wooden item into a tub of chemicals. This process often ruins the piece, drying out the wood and dissolving the glue in the joints. The old-fashioned way is the best. Use a heavy, water-soluble stripper, follow

the manufacturer's directions and *suffer*!

When deciding whether or not to strip, remember that what is wrong with the old finish may not be obvious or necessarily involve only the last coat. The wood may have been haphazardly prepared and the paint poorly applied, or someone with good intentions may have used the wrong product. If you feel that the paint surface of your project is stable, then sand it, wash it with nonphosphorus soap, and patch and spot prime it as needed. Remember to sand glossy surfaces well, especially all of the nooks and crannies.

Finally, a word of caution regarding varnished surfaces. These surfaces can be painted over after they have been properly sanded and cleaned as described above. But as it is true for any previously painted surface, the danger can lurk somewhere underneath the final coat. Even a coat of varnish over the same type of varnish that has not been properly sanded and cleaned can cause sudden blistering and cracking. Be particularly critical of any previously varnished surface.

Sample Boards— Practice, Practice, Practice

It is a good idea to prepare a sample surface to practice on before attempting the actual wall or piece of furniture. Walls are fine to practice on. However, you may wish to start on smaller boards since they are moveable and make good reference samples.

Years ago, I went through the cumbersome and futile exercise of painting sections of plywood and wallboard. (Speaking of suffering!) Imagine carrying these mammoth pieces around to show to your clients. Now I use smooth drawing or mat board. A 10″ × 15″ (25cm × 37.5cm) section of an all-media, hot-press board such as Crescent #20 is a good and reasonably priced choice. These boards are only samples so you don't need to prime them unless you seek to be a puritan. If you do want to prime them, use a PVA primer and then basecoat each board with your paint.

*G*lazes are paints that have been made glasslike or transparent by adding a glazing liquid. In other words, they are paints with a higher than normal ratio of vehicle to pigment. The more glazing liquid that is added, the greater the transparency. A vehicle such as oil, acrylic, petroleum or egg binds the powdered pigments to turn them into paint. Glazes are applied over dry undercoats and manipulated while wet to create patterns or designs. The possibilities are endless depending on the color combinations, tools, techniques and layers of glaze you use.

As with most paints, glazes consist of very few ingredients and, once you have a good formula, are easy to make. To make a glaze or paint, purchase your favorite colors of powdered pigments. Add the powdered pigments to your preferred vehicle. This vehicle, which binds and transports the pigments, can be vegetable-based (such as flax, poppy or sunflower); oil-based; latex or synthesized oil-based polymer; an egg; milk; or glue.

Depending on the type of paint, you can add refined citrus, oil or pine sap as well as water, but not too much water—it alone will break down the paint. Though the pigment will be transparent it will not bind properly.

You can add a dash of dryer, an additive that will promote curing and speed drying time of oil- or alkyd-based paints. In other cases, you can add something to keep the product from deteriorating or spoiling too quickly. There you have it, a good paint. The proper ratio of all these ingredients is the key to the paint's quality and longevity. More pigment will make the product denser. Too much will make it dry, eventually causing it to flake off. But if you add more of the complete and compatible vehicle, the paint will again become transparent—a fine, properly binding and quality glaze.

After some research and experimentation, you can make your own organic or natural paints and glazes with relative ease. While few artists do so now, many did so in the past due to preference or necessity. However, the petrol-chemical industry has given us chemically altered crude oils, plastics and polymers, which in turn give us synthetic latex (rubber) and man-made "plant oil" to use in making our paints. As a result, this industry has made us, the painters, largely dependent on their products. While it is relatively easy to make your own organic paint, it is much more difficult to make your own synthetic paint—that is, unless you are a hobby chemist or know someone with the key to the medicine cabinet. So making effective changes in these popular products to suit our needs or the environmental needs of a particular project is virtually impossible. This is not a complaint, but a sad, unchanging fact. So we must learn to work within these realities.

Luckily, the same basic rules govern all paints. For example, add glazing liquid to a paint, and you will have a glaze. The more you add, the more transparent the glaze will be. Likewise, you may add pigment to a glazing liquid and create a glaze. If you add more pigment, it will become a more or less viable paint.

Now it becomes really confusing. Although all acrylic glazing liquids are, in a sense, created equal, some are made of finer ingredients, for instance, cosmetic-grade polymers. Even more importantly, some have a retarding agent built into the formula to achieve longer open time. This is a crucial aspect of paint products, especially for the faux finisher and those working on large areas such as walls. In the case of acrylics, a retarder or extender will give you a little more time to manipulate the glaze. This is good! However, the manufacturers do not usually inform you of how much their product has been retarded.

Now if we add even more extender (I dislike the term "retarder"), we may actually extend the product to the point that it breaks down. The paint or glaze does not cure properly, if at all, and ultimately fails. Flaking, peeling and alligatoring are the results. Generally, I would recommend using a straightforward polyvinyl-based glazing medium, varnish, wallpaper size or acrylic paint additive, to which you are free (within certain limits) to add as much extender as you want.

So how much extender do you add? That depends on the products you use and the effect you wish to create. If you use a good-quality, extender-free glazing liquid, you can mix 50 percent of your glazing liquid with 40 percent extender and 10 percent water. Henceforth, this mix will be referred to as our customized glazing liquid.

Several manufacturers offer ready-to-use tinted glazes. Unfortunately, most of them are rather weak for many faux finish effects. If you want to experiment with such products, be sure that they offer suitable colorants so you can add pigments to create more opaqueness or alter the color.

Always test unfamiliar products. Experiment with different mixes and put them through a tough test. When they are dry, check their adhesion. When they are cured, wash them, scrub them, abuse them. Do not hope for the best—imitate how they'll hold up in real life.

When ready, there is no need to mix enough paint to cover a barn when you are only decorating an out-house. However, it's better to mix a little too much than to run out and have to remix the paint and the glaze.

Since a glaze is more liquid, it will coat a larger area than paint will. So if the label on the paint can promises to cover 250 to 350 square feet per gallon, a glaze may give you 350 to 500 square feet of coverage and perhaps even more.

When treating a $12' \times 15'$ room, I may mix three-fourths of a gallon of my customized glazing liquid and extender to the same amount of paint. This yields one-and-a-half gallons of glaze and leaves me with one to two quarts for touch-up, or possibly enough to redo an entire wall if necessary. Keep in mind that purchasing half or three-fourths of a gallon of paint will cost as much as or more than buying one gallon. In this case, being conservative is not always the prudent choice.

APPLYING A GLAZE

Part 1

EASY FAUX
FINISH TECHNIQUES

A natural sponge is the preferred tool for all sponging techniques. Artificial sponges do not absorb paint well. More importantly, they do not give the desired spotted image due to their straight cut and limited flexibility. Use them for cleaning your sink or floor—that is what they are made for.

Select the sponge according to the pattern you would like to produce. A section of the sponge will make contact with the surface, "printing" a pattern. For treating a large surface such as a wall, select a well-rounded one that is about the size of your hand and has a fine, even texture.

Submerge the sponge in the paint and work the paint into it by squeezing the sponge, eliminating some but not all of the paint. Use your practice board to get a feel for the amount of wetness you need and how much water or glazing liquid is required to make the paint pliable. Massage the sponge lightly to insure that the media are evenly dispersed. Have a rag ready to wipe off excess paint that has squished through your fingers or, better yet, learn to work this paint into the sponge. No dripping on the wall now, okay?

To sponge on, lightly dab the sponge onto the surface. As you continue, rotate the sponge, occasionally squeezing it lightly to work the paint into the surface of the sponge. If the sponge gives you an undesirable or unattractive pattern, rotate it more often, try another side or discard it and regroup. A slight change in the contact area may result in a dramatic change, or at least in a better image.

Avoid working in a spiral direction off of a central point. This may cause an uneven result as the sponge becomes drier. Then, after reloading your sponge, you will have a dark image next to a faint image. It is important to develop an eye for the point when you need to add paint to the sponge, avoiding such dark/light inconsistency. Work the sponge by dabbing loosely and then filling in. Try to create as uniform a pattern as possible.

To effectively deal with sponging in corners and tight spots, use a sliver of sponge to fill in where the larger tool is not effective. Don't squeeze and force the large sponge into small crevices.

First you need to master your control over the medium and tools. When you have done so, you can still be creative. Creativity without control is chaos, or at best, an accident that is difficult to repeat over the rest of your surface. It is best if the sponge and painter are constant throughout the project. People and sponges vary in the patterns they create together. Also, mix enough paint for the whole project. Make it easy on yourself. The job itself is usually enough of a challenge without adding more difficulties through improper or careless preparation.

There are endless possibilities to consider. When dry, a second color can be applied or two colors can be applied simultaneously. But keep it simple at the beginning and find time to play on the sample boards before attacking a large room.

Materials

- natural sea sponge
- gloves
- paint
- water

Sponging On

1 Select a natural sea (wool) sponge of suitable texture. Saturate the sponge and squeeze out the excess paint. Begin sponging by gently dabbing the sponge onto the prepared surface. Address no more than two to three square feet at a time. Rather than sponging in a concentric circle from the center, dab randomly at first, then begin filling the area until you have created your desired texture. If the texture appears repetitious, slightly rotate the sponge as you proceed.

2 Reload the sponge as necessary to create an evenly rough stipple effect throughout. If fast-drying paint sets up in the sponge, rinse it out, dry on a rag and continue. Upon completing a larger area, step back and review your work. Fill in by gently sponging into larger negative or open areas, thus creating a relatively even, allover texture.

3 Although some may find blotchy surface treatments desirable, most will agree that such images impress primarily by appearing amateurish and even ugly.

4 Even, allover tranquil textures are usually preferred.

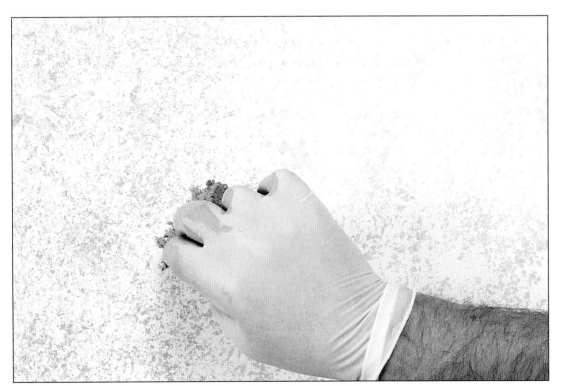

5 When dry, a second or even third shade or color may be added. This treatment can be harmonious or even contrasting, but do not overpower the first color. This may be done with the same sponge or, for further contrast, with one of a different texture.

This is a delightful variation of sponging on. It does, however, require more effort. Basically, a coat of glaze is applied to a dry base coat, then partially removed with sponges to reveal the base color or colors. This is done by alternately applying and removing the glaze with a sponge. Your imagination sets the boundaries. The secrets to success are speed and confidence, which are gained through work and practice. Work on your practice boards or try a closet first.

With this technique, using the same color in different values is usually very successful. For example, a deep forest green over a medium moss green produces a rich surface treatment. Two colors of lighter value such as a soft pink and mellow yellow-green that are applied and blended in one application over a white base will produce a delicate result and appear impressionistic, somewhat like the paintings of Claude Monet.

Establish a good system before you begin. Think about the area to be sponged. If the wall is small, maybe a 4' × 5' (3.5m × 4.5m) area, and you're only applying one color, apply a coat of glaze onto the surface using a low-nap or sponge roller. When applying two colors simultaneously, it is best to use brushes so the colors can be blended more easily. This blending can be done by using a dry sponge (about 3" × 5" or 7.5cm × 12.5cm) and dabbing the surface as in sponging on. This is not to be done for the visual effect, but to eliminate brushstrokes and guarantee a more uniform coat of glaze on the surface. It also helps to create a more refined transition between color areas.

Now you have something to work with. Immerse a different sponge of the same size into uncolored glazing liquid. Squeeze it out thoroughly so that it is only damp. Then sponge the surface, working over a small, manageable area until the glaze opens and the colored glaze begins to loosen, and you start to see the undercoat shining through. If a stronger reaction is needed, use alcohol to dissolve the glaze. Realize that this opening action is a delayed one and will take some time to happen. Be sure to

Materials

- natural sea sponges (two damp, two dry)
- colored glaze
- denatured or rubbing alcohol

have a dry sponge available to pick up any excess glazing liquid and to sponge off further as desired. Keep this sponge dry by occasionally wrapping it in a dry rag and squeezing it out.

Now move on to another area, eventually working your way over the whole wall. Reload your sponge when it no longer opens the glaze but begins removing it. Move loosely and randomly between areas, keeping the boundaries between areas wet

Sponging Off (one color)

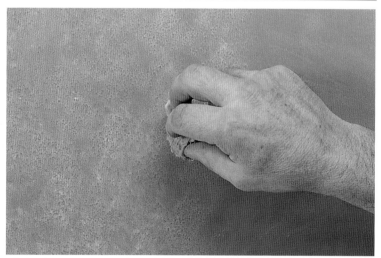

1 Apply an even coat of your choice of colored glaze. Do not seek coverage; you must always remember that a glaze is a naturally transparent medium. It is not your average paint. Immediately sponge the glazed area with a dry, natural sea sponge to create a relatively even film and texture.

and workable. Don't stay too long in one space because you may overwork an area while neglecting another. Essentially, you need to work the clear glaze into the colored glaze, thereby loosening and dissolving it. If this process does not create the effect you want and you desire a more open pattern, try a third—or fourth or fifth—sponge that has been loaded with a thinned glazing liquid. You will develop your own rhythm with experience. Again, you need to practice, practice, practice.

When attacking a large room, you may want to enlist the help of a kind volunteer or disgruntled relative. Together you can develop a good working system, for example, if your volunteer or co-worker applies the glaze, you can manipulate it. Be sure not to change roles during this process. First apply a coat of glaze to the surface as described earlier, working with a sensibly sized area and then moving on. You may apply the glaze to one third of the wall, from top to bottom, manipulating all of the area to which you have applied the glaze. Don't leave a "dead area" that has not been manipulated. Then apply the glaze to the second third of the wall, overlapping three to six inches into the previously worked area. Concentrate on the overlapping area first to properly blend these two sections so that the boundary is not evident. Finally, move on to the next third. When working over a large surface, work as quickly as possible, keeping all areas wet so you can come back and rework the whole surface, creating a uniform pattern throughout the room.

The finished surface will take a month to cure even though it may feel dry to the touch in less than twenty-four hours. The surface of an acrylic-based paint may feel perfectly dry after a very short time. But proper curing time—the point when the paint reaches maximum strength—is actually two to four weeks.

2 Saturate a small section of the sea sponge in denatured or rubbing alcohol. Wring it out until it is damp. Gently and randomly sponge the alcohol into the glaze, closing the contact points as you go. Realize that alcohol dissolves acrylics, but the interaction between it and the glaze is delayed. So do not overwork or oversaturate the area.

3 As the alcohol opens up the glaze, sponge off with a damp and a dry sponge. Again, work the glaze gently. You wish to create texture, not remove most or all of the medium. Should an area run or sag, dry it with a dry sponge. If required, rinse the sponges in water or alcohol.

4 An area that becomes too light may be darkened by sponging in a little color. Integrate it immediately by sponging off. Repeat by treating an area completely, or partially, as needed to create a generally even, cloudlike, allover texture.

Sponging Off (one color, wet-into-dry)

Acrylics have a notably short open time (the period of time a medium can be manipulated). Thus, you must devise methods to avoid buildup of materials where the drying edges and wetter work areas meet. For example, say you have completed a 6′ × 8′ (5.5m × 7.5m) area. When the adjoining field is coated, it will naturally overlap into the previous (now dry) field.

One Color, Wet-Into-Dry

♦ colored glaze

♦ clean brush or fine roller

♦ clear glazing medium

1 With a clean rag, brush or fine roller, apply a thin coat of clear glazing medium to the perimeter of or the entire section you will be working. A blend of about 50 percent glazing liquid, 40 percent extender and 10 percent water should serve you well. Apply your colored glaze to the space within. Be sure to blend it well at the outer edges with the wet clear liquid. Feather it out at the perimeter by drybrushing. Treat as previously in sponging off.

2 The adjoining area is integrated by first applying the clear glaze and then overlapping into the faded outer edges of the previously textured area. Also, extend the border regions of this new section. Apply your colored glaze within this space and into the finished, yet weak regions. Blend well.

3 Begin sponging off by blending in the border areas, where wet and dry meet. Extend the sponged areas to also fade out toward the section to be textured next. The borders should not be treated as rigid, like squares, but as somewhat organic.

4 When finished, the entire area should appear even-textured, even if cloudy.

Sponging Off (two colors)

1 This is simply an extension of the previous treatments. Here, two different-colored glazes are used and simultaneously applied. One brush should be used for each color to keep these colors pure but well-blended at the perimeter.

Materials

Two Colors

♦ two different colors of glaze
♦ two brushes (one for each color)
♦ denatured or rubbing alcohol
♦ several natural sea sponges

2 The individual, colored glaze areas should not be painted too rigidly. They should appear to be abstract or esoteric, intermingling shapes of pure and well-blended colors. Refine by further blending when dry sponging.

3 Begin sponging in the alcohol. Here it is important to use several sponges, each used in only one of the colors. This will ensure that no one color of glaze is transferred into another.

4 Again, dry sponges are used to lift out the glaze that was dissolved by the alcohol. Do not overwork; create a more or less smooth interplay of all colors with one another and with the base.

5 The finished project should display a cloudy, shapeless, balanced texture and a gentle exchange of shades of colors and transparencies. The base color should glow through the glazes.

Effective Corner Treatment

1 An often-asked question is how to treat corners and ceiling lines. The most awful mistake painters make is to force a sponge or rag into corners and tight areas. This practice makes it appear as if ugly skid marks are framing the surface or wall area.

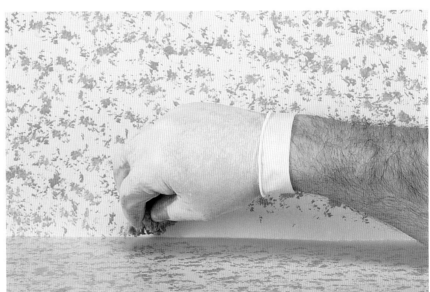

2 Sponge an area as usual. Texture the surface as close as you dare to the corners and ceiling lines without touching any surface past the corner and without forcing yourself to work too close. Being careful not to overwork, use a very small section of the sponge and gently dab into the corners.

This technique is related to sponging on, but uses rags rather than sponges. However, the visual effect is not at all the same as when using a sponge. Burlap, cheesecloth or even soft leather can be used. I like to work with cotton rags, either knitted material such as T-shirts or woven fabric such as bedsheets. The woven rags give a crisp, more attractive image. Avoid using synthetic fibers in any cloth since they repel the liquid. Use natural fibers instead.

There are two basic ragging on techniques. In both, the rag is saturated with the glaze as in sponging on. In the version the British use most, the rag is loosely folded to a sausage-shaped five-inch length, then given a moderate twist on both ends in opposite directions. This sausage-shaped rag is then rolled onto the surface. This method works well on small areas or in bands where it gives an interestingly flowing, fabriclike pattern. But when it is used on larger areas, it is difficult to control. The rag becomes hard to manipulate as it folds up or falls apart, and the pattern can appear tracklike.

For most applications, the Central European or Continental method is a better choice. The rag is casually bundled into a loose ball and then gently rolled over the surface. The direction of the rolling is generally upward but may be moved in any direc-

tion. The rag is worked with both hands and rolled over the surface. The rag ball is rotated within itself using your fingers. As the rag is rotated, fresh paint is introduced onto the surface, resulting in an ever-changing pattern. With practice, this will produce an even pattern.

With the Continental method, you must learn to judge when to reload the rag. You also need to keep a loose hand on the rag and avoid pressing too hard or allowing the rag to become too dry, which can create an undesirable fabriclike imprint. If

an area appears too open with no imprint, you can dab here and there to fill in. Or if an area is too dense, allow it to dry and rag in a little base color.

Materials

Ragging On (British)

- three-foot square rag made from a cotton bedsheet
- paint or glaze
- gloves

Ragging On (British)

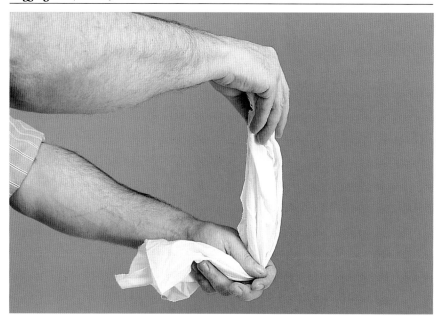

1 Select about a three-foot-square section of material without seams or undesirable texture. Saturate it completely in your paint or glaze, which should be about the consistency of heavy cream. Squeeze the rag out, wipe off your gloves and follow with another gentler squeeze. This distributes the medium equally throughout the rag.

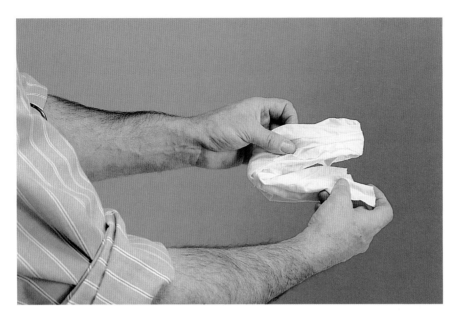

2 Open the rag completely, then gather it in extending folds from the top. Straighten out these folds and fold the rag lengthwise into three or four "sausages" between four and six inches long.

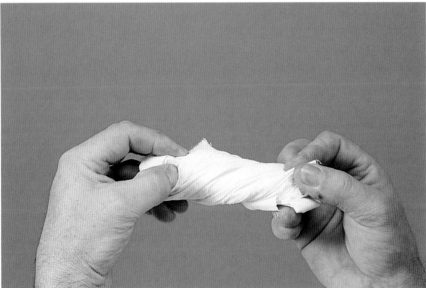

3 Hold on to both ends of the rag and give it a good twist. The folds in this twist will determine the texture.

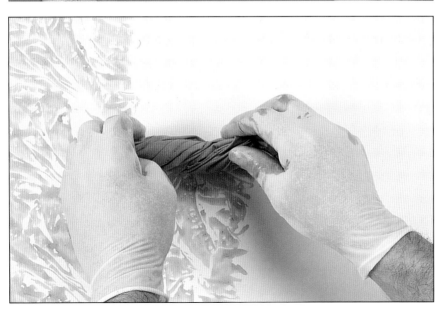

4 Now roll the rag over the surface while maintaining the twist. This is not an easy matter. These "sausages" simply do not like to cooperate. The rag must remain gathered as well as sharply twisted, all while even pressure is distributed throughout and the rag is rolled.

5 As you properly roll the rag forward and upward over the surface, a wonderful, flowing fabric texture is being created. However, a definite and not always desirable pattern emerges: The rolled bands are often distinctly defined. Also, as medium is rolled out of the rag, the texture becomes weaker. Thus, this technique is best saved for small areas only.

Ragging On (Continental, two colors)

1 More practical and far easier to execute is the Continental method of ragging on. Here the saturated, squeezed out rag is completely opened up. It is then simply left to fall from one hand into the other.

Materials

Continental, One or Two Colors

♦ cotton rag

♦ two different colors of paint or glaze

This technique will form a loose ball.

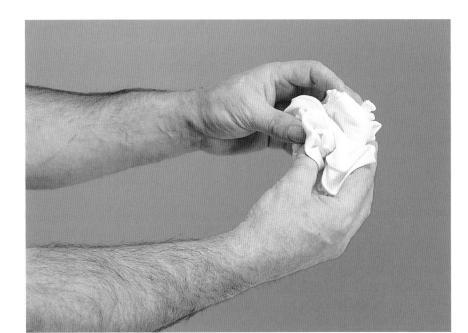

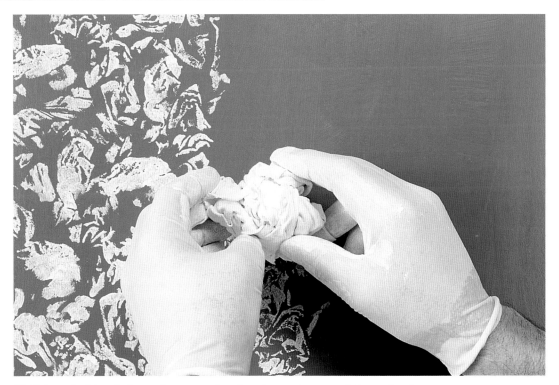

2 This rag ball is rolled over the prepared surface. Just as the rag and the medium's consistency determine the texture, so does the pressure you use. Therefore, moderate, even pressure is recommended. The saturated rag should easily "print" a clear texture. If it does not, it probably means the rag is too dry or the medium is too thick.

3 Generally, it is best to roll the rag upward, so sections of the rag do not fall out of your fingers or make undesired contact with the surface. Slight rolling sideways is appropriate so the pattern does not become too rigid. The expanding texture will need to fill any cavity.

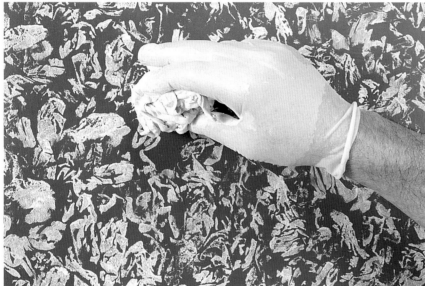

4 Any offending open area can be filled by gently dabbing a small amount of medium into it, so it becomes a harmonious part of the whole.

5 The completed surface should have a generally even, allover texture.

6 When the first medium is dry, a second or even third color may be rag-rolled over the first.

7 Again, offending cavities are textured by gently dabbing medium into them.

8 Colors may be shades of the same color or complementary accents. Harsh, conflicting color choices are perhaps best reserved for public places. The finished project is best when the texture is consistent and balanced.

Ragging On (correcting mistakes)

1 Most offending blotchy areas are spots where you have "parked" much too long. Perhaps you needed a break and conversation, but then forgot to remove your rag from the wall. Perhaps you simply pushed a bit too hard or had too much medium on the rag. First, do not wipe. Let the paint dry.

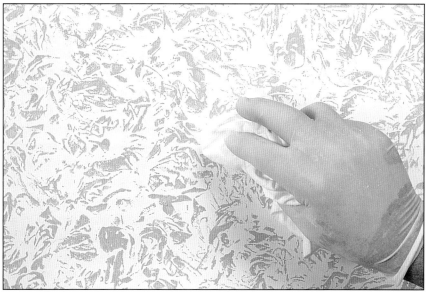

2 Use a rag that has been saturated with your paint medium—in this case, the base color. Dab gently into the offending spot. This will break up the image and integrate it into the remaining texture.

3 The wound is now mended and the project saved. However, this must be avoided at all costs. It is more desirable to first practice, practice, practice on sample boards or in your basement.

*R*agging off is less labor-intensive than sponging off and is often used for accent treatments. It can be the basis for more complicated techniques such as marbling.

Apply a glaze over the undercoat. Then, as in ragging on, gather the rag but do not add tinted glaze. Roll it through the glaze *clean*. Change and rearrange the rag as necessary.

Applying a satin-sheen paint over the undercoat as your base will allow for better pickup. You may wish to rag off two or three times in various directions. If you roll a rag that has been dampened with plain glazing liquid over the rag-rolled surface, the liquid will break through the glaze that has already set up in the pattern of the rag. Rolling over it again with a dry rag will pick up this loosened glaze and create more pattern.

You can also apply a second color of glaze. The second glaze is most effective if it is more transparent than the first glaze, allowing the first treatment to shine through.

Materials

Ragging Off (Continental or British)

♦ glaze
♦ brush for applying glaze
♦ cotton knit or linen rags for removing glaze

Ragging Off (Continental or British)

1 Paint your choice of glaze onto the surface using a brush or other preferred painting implement. (When applying glazes to a surface, use a brush to cut in and a brush or roller for the general area, depending on the size of the project. When working on larger areas, consider the wet-edge, clear glazing medium treatment mentioned under "Sponging Off, wet-into-dry" on page 24.)

2 This is a negative broken color technique, since medium is removed instead of being applied. Clean, dry rags are required. Cotton knit or linen are good choices. As in the positive technique, roll the rag through the wet medium, thus removing it from the areas of direct contact.

3 Review and improve the finished area by gentle dabbing it. Within the natural restrictions of acrylic's open time, both the Continental and British techniques work well. However, it is suggested that you choose less ambitious projects until you have gained some experience and thus speed.

Mottling is a good technique to use when an antiqued effect is desired. Leather, fabric and cloud effects may be achieved depending on the colors, materials and glaze composition used in the mottling.

Traditionally, the colored glaze was applied over the dry base. Then a cotton rag or mutton cloth was pounced over the surface until a gentle, nearly undetectable transition of color between the base color and glaze color was achieved, and a fine film of glaze remained. Today, more defined images are fashionable.

Have plenty of cotton knit rags available—six to ten pounds per room. This type of rag can be purchased at your paint store. To start, apply the glaze over the dried base. Then pounce over the surface with a dry, roughly balled up rag. Avoid overworking at this time. Work in a loose pattern over as large an area as possible.

The best results from mottling come from going over the surface at least three times. The first pass breaks open the glaze to reveal some of the base, and the second pass catches the runs. Some of the details should be of the pure glaze colors, while others should show the glaze-tinted base color.

Now to the third pass—fine mottling. Make sure that you use a clean rag for this pass, since the goal will be to lightly blend the glaze and not to transpose it. Bunch the rag into a smooth ball, not the rough ball used earlier. Hold the rag smooth surface out, and hit it on the palm of your hand once or twice to create a flatter surface. Now gently mottle the glaze by pouncing the flattened rag over the surface. It is important that the surface of your rag be fairly clean. Vary the pressure you use to create the desired transition of color: More pressure will lift the glaze and less pressure will result in a gentler transition of color. Again, be critical. Step back and view the overall effect, fine tuning as necessary.

As discussed earlier, develop a logical system for treating large walls. If another person is working with you, make certain that your co-worker does one step while you do the other. For example, if your co-worker applies the glaze, then you do the mottling, and vice versa, taking turns until the project is complete. This gives you two pairs of eyes to examine the work and make corrections. Even though this is a cooperative effort, it is usually best if one person is in charge and this should be decided before starting the project.

Multiglazes work well using this technique. The second and third glazes should not dominate the first effect, but should be used as accents. Wipe on a thin coat of clear glazing liquid and mottle color into this glaze.

Materials

- ♦ glaze
- ♦ brush or roller for applying glaze
- ♦ cotton knit rags

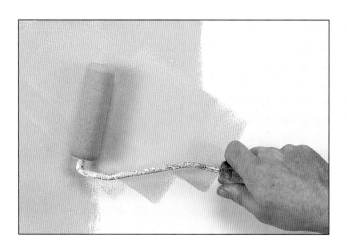

Mottling

1 This is a traditional English technique that is often described as a leather effect. Usually a glaze is applied over a base and mottled (or modeled) with a cotton knit rag to create an even, transparent glow. Modern application does prefer a subtle-to-obvious cloudy texture in which the base more or less glows through the glaze.

2 Mottle or pounce the entire area, first somewhat randomly and all over, and then close the texture pattern. To assure that consistency becomes the hallmark of your finished product, this type of control and quality must be maintained from the start.

3 Form a pounce by using a clean cotton knit rag formed into a ball. This time, however, an outer layer of the rag needs to cover it. Gather the rag in the back and flatten the ball a bit by hitting it into the palm of your hand.

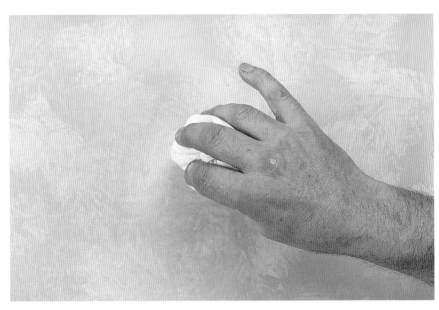

4 Pounce as before. Now, however, you need to eliminate as much of the texture as possible. Since some of this texture is likely to remain, it is important to mottle randomly at first and then close the texture pattern. Be careful not to overwork one area in favor of another.

5 If you concentrate too much on one area, you will neglect other sections, which have a limited open time. As a result, your best efforts will look amateurish. Your finished product should resemble the texture of a fine leather or that of an exquisite, handmade paper.

Mottling to Create a Textured Finish

1 Apply your glaze with a brush or roller over the base coat. Again, a wet base or perimeter may aid in creating a uniform texture on larger areas. Do not look for "good" coverage. This is, after all, a glaze, and is transparent by nature and design. First mottle rather roughly by dabbing a crumpled up cotton knit rag ball into the glaze. Be very active in this pursuit and careful not to overwork an area. Be loose—a little dab here and there, then some more here. Don't remove all of the glaze, but give the entire area a rough, cloudy appearance.

2 Now form a cotton knit rag into a pounce. Do this by balling the rag up and giving it a smooth, tight outer layer. In other words, a single or double layer of the rag covers the crumpled ball. Hold it rather tightly, then flatten it somewhat by hitting the pounce into the palm of your hand.

Materials

Textured Finish

♦ glaze
♦ brush or roller for applying glaze
♦ cotton knit rags

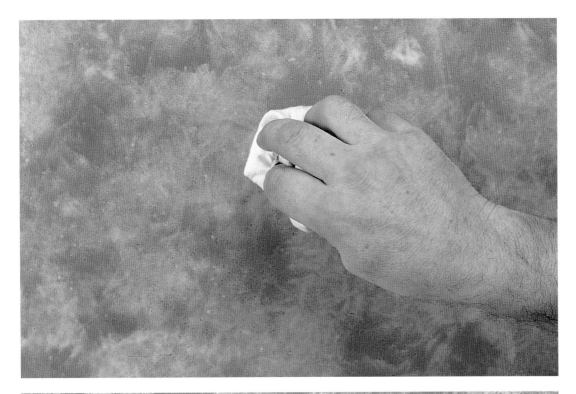

3 Now gently soften the rough mottled images by softly pouncing the surface. This treatment must be selective, not all over. Lighten the light areas, removing the most evident rag marks. Soften the texture around the dark areas and very tenderly break into the pure color glaze images, giving them an uneven, slight transparency.

Options are nearly as plentiful as the proverbial pebbles on a beach. Here a lavender base was overglazed and mottled in a Mediterranean green color. Generally, darker colored glazes work better over lighter bases, creating a certain blush or backlighting effect. Reversed, the effect can be somewhat milky—at worst, some may call it swamp water.

Optional color

Traditional finish

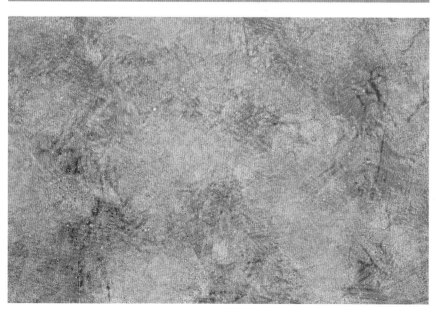

Generally preferred finish (textured)

Mottling With Overglaze

1 Any of the basic broken color techniques will yield unlimited variations and decorative possibilities. For instance, you can use two different colors of glaze in our mottling technique. You can, of course, apply both simultaneously over the base, much as was illustrated earlier in the section on sponging off.

Materials

With Overglaze

◆ two different colors of glaze

◆ brush or roller for applying glazes

◆ cotton knit rag

◆ housepainting brush

◆ clear glazing medium

2 However, by mottling the colors in separate applications, you will be able to explore a new arena of possibilities. In this example, a dark green glaze is applied over a burgundy-colored satin-sheen base. The surface is mottled as described earlier and left to dry.

3 The finished first glaze should display such a high degree of craftsmanship that it could be the final treatment. An overglaze, delicate or boorish, will not and should not hide any sin. The glaze should be adequately cured within twelve to forty-eight hours, depending on the weather conditions. Do not proceed until the surface is free of "tack."

4 The overglazing is simply a repetition of the first technique over the first glaze with, of course, another color. When doing so, as in this example, the gold color dominates and overpowers all previous work. It creates what some will consider an undesirable "swamp water" effect.

5 Here you'll utilize a system that was explored in an earlier technique—working into a clear wet base. This allows you the luxury of maximum control over exactly how much color is added. Using a housepainting brush, apply a thin coat of clear glazing medium—50 percent glazing liquid, 40 percent extender, 10 percent water—to a manageable section of the surface.

6 In this example, a gold-colored (not metallic) glaze was blended into the clear wet glazing medium. This should be done with purpose in strategic areas in order to complement, not overpower, the earlier mottled effect. Blend the edges of the gold-colored clouds and feather them into the wet base. Even now, at this early stage, the images should appear gentle, not crass.

7 Tenderly mottle the gold to create pure and ghostly cloudlike images. They should appear to float in and over the red and green previously textured surface.

8 In the finished product, the last gold-colored glaze appears as an equal to the previous dark green glaze and burgundy base. In most cases, however, it may prove more exquisite and elegant if it is used with discretion. In the case of color, at least, too much of a good thing can appear vulgar and garish. A discreet hint or nuance can proclaim style and class.

A wash, or French wash, is a version of an effect traditionally created by using *distemper* paint, which is an old, environment-friendly paint consisting of glue, water, chalk and pigment. Mixed in the proper proportions, it held up well under most conditions. This paint let the surface breathe, but it remained water-soluble and was susceptible to moisture damage. Under good conditions, it lasted a long time, but since it could not be washed, repainting was necessary every three to six years. The old paint was washed off, and the surface repainted. The surface commonly treated was plaster or cement, and there were often faint streaks and swirls left after the washing, especially if the painters were amateurish and the surface was not thoroughly cleaned between paintings. Residue would often be washed up from previous paintings.

Thus, a French wash is essentially an attempt to create a surface that looks as if the distemper paint was partially removed prior to repainting. It can also be a recreation of weatherworn or sunbeaten exterior walls found in Mediterranean villages. This look can be interesting with the right choice of colors.

Since this technique is rather active, avoid hot and aggressive colors. Using a few drops of Raw or Burnt Umber is always helpful. Keep the colors light and/or thin, warm and somewhat earthy. You may choose a principle color and one or two accent colors that have been thinned or made into a glaze.

Wet the wall first with a thinned glazing liquid, then randomly brush in the different-colored glazes, distressing in all possible directions. Most painters use a larger short or worn-down white-bristled paintbrush. Since this is a somewhat wild technique, you may want to work with a brush in each hand. I prefer brushing on the glaze, taking a knit rag or burlap and, at first gently, then with a little more force, wiping in the pattern by removing the glaze. Wipe in loose, short, curved strokes. Backhand the surface by taking the rag in one corner and smacking it against the surface. Or bunch the rag into a ball and give it a swirl, or hold it loosely and wipe. Wiping with the rag will give you a nice effect.

Since the surface we are trying to emulate was created with a water-based distemper paint, it is logical that water-based products can easily be used here. Distemper paint is the best and easiest paint to use for this technique and can be varnished for practical reasons. However, acrylic or latex paints are more commonly used and readily available. The brushing technique works best with these products since the paint sets up faster and does not respond as well to the rag movements. You may wish to "torture" your brush by using the sides of the bristles, or try using an old broom or scrub brush.

Since this is an extremely wet technique requiring the use of copious amounts of water, be sure to carefully cover the floor. Have a little workout and a lot of fun!

Materials

- two or more different colors of glaze
- clear glazing medium
- white bristle strié brush, wallpapering brush or feather duster
- white bristle ring brush (or bristle softener)
- a rag made of cotton knit, cheesecloth or burlap

Wash

1 The wash—at times called the French wash—is often said to imitate the weatherworn exterior of a Mediterranean lime stucco facade. Its execution is actually quite simple. Apply two or more different colors of glaze to a dry base or a base dampened with a clear glazing medium.

2 Since this type of broken color technique is very active, it may work best if somewhat earthy, less active colors are used. Blend these colors well at the perimeter, and occasionally work in a little extra glazing liquid or water. This will ensure variable transparency, texture and opaqueness.

3 Traditionally, paste or distemper paint brushes with white, black, or calcutta bristles are used to first apply, then texture the glazes. Natural plant fiber lime brushes are also used. (Those traditional tools are not obsolete, and, in fact, are very much required in marble and wood imitations.) Today anything similar, such as a white bristle strié wallpapering brush or duster, may be found useful. Such a brush is whisked through the wet glaze to create a distressed texture.

4 A white bristle ring brush or bristle softener can aid in refining the effect. These tools may be used rather roughly, which goes against my usual recommendations.

5 If any of the aforementioned brushes are not available or if you just want to try something different, you may use a rag. Cotton knit, cheesecloth or burlap will do just fine. Whisk the rag with more or less pressure through the glaze. Be lucid in your movements, scratching the surface for an allover, directional texture.

6 Stop working the glaze before it dries, since by then the texture will have become muddled and weak. Now you can understand why I consider most notions about a Mediterranean or even French wash as overly romantic. Actually, such imitations more resemble a traditional European interior surface: an aged distemper-type paint made of chalk, bone glue, pigment and water washed in preparation for repainting.

*P*ronounced *fra-tahje*, this technique is relatively quick and simple to do and yields rewarding results. Depending on the color choice and consistency of the glaze, the effect may look like marble, stone, stucco or burled wood. Again, a glaze is applied over a base coat and then lifted off. You may use crumpled up plastic trash bags to frottage the glaze. Personally, I have several favorite materials that give different effects.

Before you begin, you'll need to crumple up double sheets of newsprint, then straighten the sheets out and double them up. Doubling the paper causes it to act as a cushion, which will help you avoid heavy-handed imprints. Be sure to have enough paper already crumpled and folded to do the job. I prefer newsprint because it allows for less direct contact with the liquids. Most printing inks in use today are soy-based and soluble, causing occasional residual ink to mix into the glaze. If this is a problem, get unprinted newsprint paper.

Once you have your papers ready, apply the glaze to the surface. Place your folded paper onto the glazed surface and lightly smooth over the paper with the flat of your hand. Lift off this sheet, turn it inside out and repeat the process using the second side. When treating a small area, you may wish to frottage a second time or take a section of the crumpled paper to remove a little more from an area. When dealing with a large surface, frottage section by section in the order the glaze was applied. Overlap by a fraction each time. Avoid wiping too close to the edge of the paper as this will leave an imprint of the edge of the paper. This should not be a problem if you are working with doubled paper. You can go over the sur-

Materials

Paper

- ◆ thin, transparent glaze
- ◆ housepainting brush
- ◆ newspaper, newsprint or plastic sheeting

face a second time if the glaze has not set up or is still open. Avoid placing the paper in the same place; offset the pattern to ensure uniformity.

You can use a variety of other materials such as plastic grocery store bags or cellophane. Get out your sample boards and play. Keep the materials consistent when working over larger areas. 3M's Scotch Professional Masking Film, crumpled and bunched into a loose ball, works well. Dab it over the glazed surface, rotating and turning it inside out for better pickup.

Frottage With Newspaper

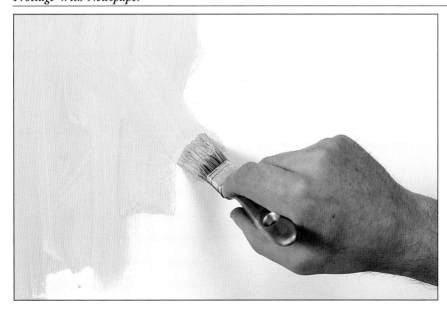

1 For best results in executing a frottage technique—or in frotting, as the English would say—a relatively thin, transparent glaze is required. In other words, more glazing liquid than usual needs to be added to the medium. Apply a coat of glaze using a practical painting implement. (When applying glazes to a surface, use a brush to cut in and a brush or roller for the general area, depending on the size of the project.)

2 Crumple up a double sheet of newsprint, squeezing it into a very tight ball. Open the sheet completely, being careful not to tear it and leaving the paper as textured as possible. If a test should prove that the ink is not stable and the resulting discoloration is undesirable, then you can use unprinted newspaper.

3 Double up the crumpled newsprint and lay it flat onto the surface and into the wet glaze. Gently smooth the paper with the flat palm and extended fingers of your hands. Here it proves helpful to have double-layered the paper, since this cushions the contact. You must execute this act carefully and gently without your fingers, palms or knuckles protruding.

4 Do not wipe to the very edge of the paper since this will most assuredly leave a line imprint. Carefully lift the paper, beginning in a top corner, completely out of the glaze. If the texture is too light, repeat by first turning it inside out, then applying it again. This helps keep your hands relatively clean and, more importantly, provides a dry paper surface for better texture.

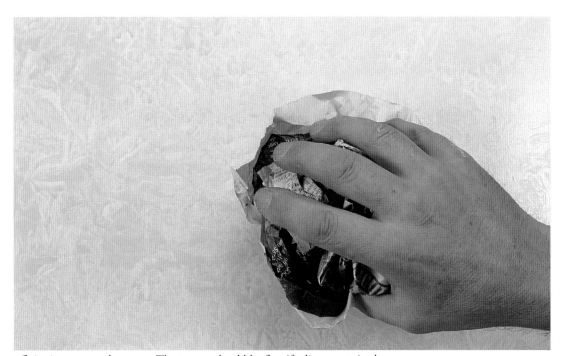

5 Again, remove the paper. The texture should be fine if adjustments in the pressure are used in smoothing the paper the second time. Any small spots or areas that still need improving and integrating can be textured with a balled up wad of paper. Be sure to rotate the ball so you do not simply disperse color.

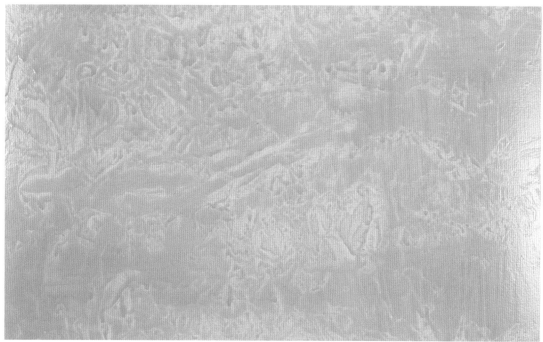

6 The finished product should be what some describe as a leatherette texture. Again, as in any broken color technique, there are options. Two colored glazes may be applied at the same time. They should be blended extremely well at the perimeters.

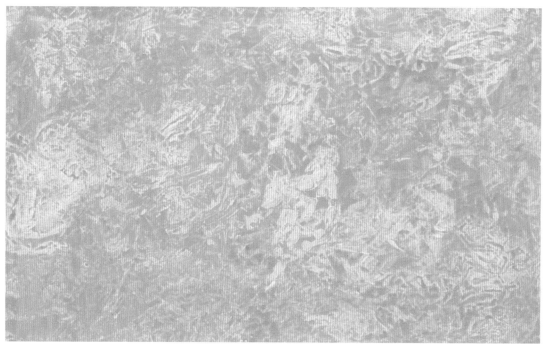

7 A frottage, of course, may also be overglazed with a second color. Here the sample was overglazed and frottaged after the first texture had dried. The rose color used here was somewhat stronger. This is a good reason to be certain that the glaze is indeed adequately transparent. Always test each process and the materials you use on a sample board.

Frottage With Plastic Wrap

Plastic Wrap

- colored glaze
- plastic wrap (from a garbage bag, shopping bag or painter's drop cloth)
- heavy glaze for "smooching method"

1 Most common plastics, such as garbage or shopping bags and painter's plastic sheeting, are used in frotting. The basic principles remain the same, as does the technical aspect. The texture, however, may vary slightly or greatly, depending on the material you use, its application and the glaze's consistency. Apply a coat of colored glaze.

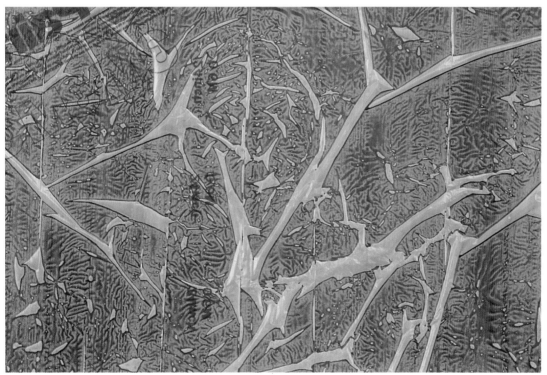

2 Different thicknesses of plastic will create varying effects. Heavier plastic logically gives less texture than thinner or lighter selections. Harder plastics will be coarser than softer varieties. "Hang" the plastic sheet into the wet glaze. You can mold the final glaze texture the same way you mold the plastic when installing it. Contact areas will become negative; noncontact areas the opposite.

3 Usually no smoothing is required when using plastic, as opposed to the newsprint technique. The plastic just wants to cling to the wet surface. Perhaps a little blowing here or there is all that is needed to attach the sheeting to the wet surface. Carefully lift the plastic off the glaze from a top corner. Generally, no second contact is required, although you may improve some areas by dabbing.

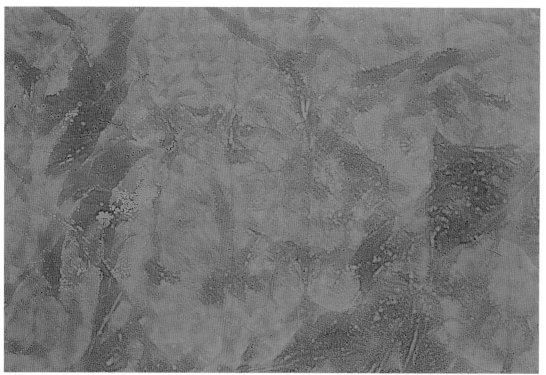

4 The finished texture should look marblelike in an abstract sort of way. Depending on the colors used, it may resemble stone or other natural or synthetic textures. The application and intermixing of two-color glazes, as well as a partial or complete overglazing, are, as always, options worth exploring.

An alternative to the aforementioned technique is what some sophisticates prefer to call "smooching." Here a heavy glaze is applied to the plastic, which is attached and moved about on the surface. The difference is rather unconvincing. Also, in many cases, this process will leave a three-dimensional texture, which is a problem in repainting efforts.

Frottage With Crumpled Cellophane

1 For a tighter if not crisper texture, use cellophane, such as masking film by 3M. Other similar materials, like cheap plastic bags, will work almost as well, at least when small amounts of materials are needed. Again, apply a moderate coating of glaze.

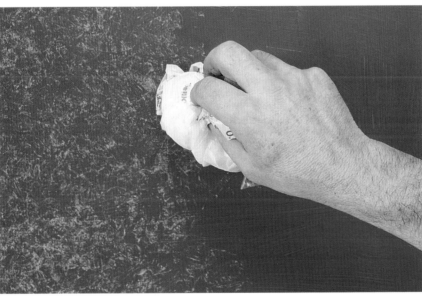

2 Crumple a section of cellophane into a ball. Since cellophanes are harder than other plastics, they crumple more easly, forming a sharper texture. Dab the cellophane ball into the wet glaze, thus creating a negative texture. Since the material needs to be rotated, you may prefer to wear plastic or rubber gloves. Dab rather randomly at first, then close the pattern to your satisfaction.

3 The final product will display a fine, tight-textured glaze. Although some may label these effects leatherette or "smooching," their traditional name is frottage or frotting. Depending on the base and glaze colors, they may imitate various stones to give slate and stucco effects.

Materials

Crumpled Cellophane

♦ cellophane (e.g., 3M's masking film)

♦ colored glaze

♦ plastic or rubber gloves

Part 2

ECLECTIC FAUX FINISH TECHNIQUES

*P*ronounced *stry-ay* in French, this term refers to the creation of a delicate (perhaps somewhat irregular) striped effect over a surface. This is a basic technique used for woodgraining. Using the proper base color, such as a pale terra-cotta with a glaze of Burnt Sienna and/or Burnt Umber, you can create a good straight-grained Philippine mahogany wood effect. An eggshell or satin-sheen base coat is necessary here.

Strié may be used for entire walls, wainscoting, furniture and other accents. Apply the glaze to the surface as usual, and then pull some type of graining tool through the glaze to create the striped effect. Drag the tool straight through the glaze from the top to the bottom. Repeat or reverse this motion until you achieve your desired effect.

The dragger is occasionally recommended for this process. It is a very thin, wide, and flat brush made of 3½- to 4-inch long gray bristles or horsehairs. However, the flogger, which is similar to the dragger, is a more versatile tool. The flogger has hairs 1- to 1½-inch longer than the dragger and is useful for many grained effects. Pull the flogger through the glaze by placing it at an angle to the surface so you can use your other hand to press down on the bristles as you move along the surface. Other brushes can be used, such as a variety of mottlers or nylon bristle over-grainers, but their success is limited to thinner glazes.

Steel or rubber combs can also be used. Cover the tool with a cheesecloth or rough rag, and pull it through the glaze. Sackcloth or cheesecloth pulled over any flat object such as cardboard can be a very useful strié tool. This technique is often used along with the dragger or flogger.

One of my tricks is to use medium-weight steel wool. I pull it through the glaze as explained above, repeating this several times in a straight line in opposite directions. On smaller areas, the result is often better than with the earlier-mentioned methods.

Materials

Traditional

- steel graining comb, or other strié tool
- glazes of Burnt Sienna and Burnt Umber
- cheesecloth
- flogger brush (optional)

Traditional Strié

1 Traditional strié effects are created with various tools. The most noted among them are the steel woodgraining combs. To create a simple woodgrain effect using this method, apply Burnt Sienna and Burnt Umber glazes in bands over a light terra-cotta-colored satin-sheen base. These colored glazes are blended where they meet to assure a fine, delicate transition of colors.

2 Drape a doubled layer of cheesecloth over a steel comb. Tuck the loose ends of the fabric away, preferably folding them to the top of the comb to avoid unwanted contact of the loose ends with the surface. Now pull the comb over the surface and through the glaze. The texture depends on the selection of the comb, the consistency of the glaze and the pressure you use.

3 The finished strié texture should run straight plumb and may be refined with the aid of a flogger brush. Floggers or draggers are pulled in the direction of the strié over and through the still-wet glaze, thus refining the texture. If you have no access to these specialty brushes, you may investigate some of the following alternatives. These could be incorporated into the combed strié technique.

Strié With Brush

1 Larger areas, such as entire walls or rooms, are best executed by a team of two painters. The first applies the glaze just ahead of the other, who executes the actual strié texturing. The most effective method is the use of a strié brush or a wide, flat, short-bristled brush like those used in smoothing wallpaper during installation. Here, to make the surface more interesting, I taped out a band of white in the otherwise medium-dark blue basecoated surface.

2 When dry, mix a gunpowder blue out of a deep Ultramarine Blue and Raw Umber, making the blue as dark as possible without losing the bluish quality. Apply a thin glaze of this color over the base and texture it with a strié brush.

Materials

With Brush

♦ strié brush or a flat, short-bristled brush such as a wallpapering brush

♦ thin, colored glaze

♦ dull enamel eggshell for base

♦ spritzer brush

3 The completed strié will reveal through the glaze the lighter blue-and-white band, a combination suitable also for furnishings. Besides changing the color and composition of the glaze itself, the effect can be adjusted by using a different base. In this example, a dull eggshell enamel was used. If this base were a satin or even semigloss sheen, more of the base colors would be revealed due to the smoothness of the first coat.

4 To create a "wormhole" effect, thin the dark blue paint with water and spatter it onto the surface with the aid of a "spritzer" brush. This is a short, round, domed white bristle brush similar to some fabric brushes. Load the brush with medium, pull the bristles back and release. This produces a spray of fine mist or speckles of color on the surface. Be sure to test it first on a practice surface to determine exactly how much medium at what consistency is needed in the bristle for proper and controlled application.

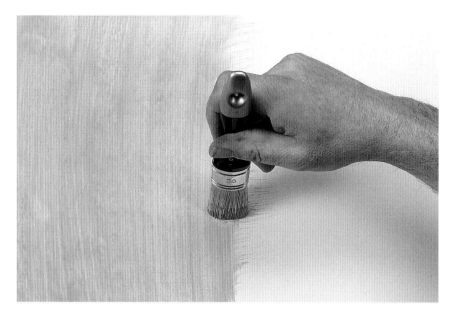

Strié With Steel Wool

1 Strié effects can be created with many "tools," such as burlap and cardboard. On a small scale and with some limitations, steel wool will create interesting strié effects. Apply a contrasting glaze onto the dry background. When you use two colors, they must be banded in the direction of the strié and well-blended where they meet.

2 Drag a pad or section of medium-coarse steel wool through the wet glaze several times. When working on areas with moldings or other obstructions, some care must be taken in getting into the corners. The sharp fold of a complete pad may help. If not, another strié method may be advisable. On unobstructed areas, however, moving the wool up and down through the medium, away from and toward your center, can produce wonderful results.

3 The resulting texture is a delightful checked strié. It is very useful for antiquing and background effects in furniture as well as moldings and railings. When employing the proper color combinations, this variety of strié will create a very realistic straight-grain mahogany as well as other wood imitations.

Materials

With Steel Wool

♦ a pad of medium-coarse steel wool (burlap fabric or cardboard may also be used)

♦ two contrasting colors of glaze

Strié With Overglaze

1 This is a possible addition to or extension of the previously described strié effects. Overglazing the first strié and repeating the texturing, even in a highly contrasting color, can be very interesting but may have only a moderate effect. So let's entertain another option. When the first glaze is dried, apply another shade or color glaze over it.

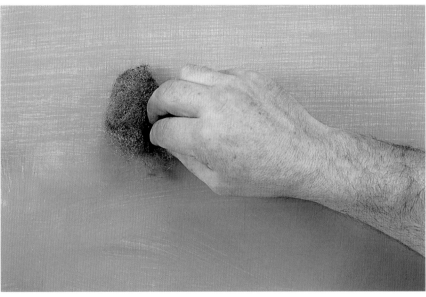

2 Treat this glaze in the same fashion as the first, except strié in the opposite direction. If the first texture was horizontal, the second should go against the grain vertically. This second glaze should generally be of the same or somewhat lighter consistency as the first to assure that it is not obliterating all of your previous efforts.

3 The final product should be a well-executed fabric imitation. Depending on the coarseness of the steel wool, fabric or brushes you used, the texture will resemble fine to coarse linen, curtain or denim fabrics, canvas or burlap.

Materials

With Overglaze

♦ a pad of medium-coarse steel wool (burlap fabric or cardboard may also be used)

♦ two contrasting colors of glaze

Artists have used brushes to stipple for as long as they have used them to paint. Stenciling (using a stippling technique) gained popularity in the fifteenth century, during which time the painter's guild considered the technique a deceitful art and condemned the practice. Stippling, however, was widely used. Painters and plasterers were members of the same guild, and so stippling found as much use in texturing plaster as in painting to imitate stone, for instance.

Thus we see a great similarity in certain brushes that painters and plasterers traditionally use. This often leads to misunderstanding the purpose of one brush in comparison to another, and why one is preferred over another. Although some plaster brushes are round and made of natural fibers, most stipple brushes are made of white or Calcutta (gray) bristles. They all resemble a traditional push broom in that bundles of fiber or bristle are set into a round, square or rectangular plate.

One brush that is often sold as a stippler is the standard European paste or paintbrush. Realize that a high-grade stippler is worth about three times the cost of the same-quality paste brush, and the paintbrush is not designed to do the job properly. The plate of the paste or paintbrush measures about 4″ × 6″, and has finer bristles than those of the stippler, for which only the strongest hair is selected. A stippler's hair is generally shorter than those of its cousins, and the hair is set in tighter bundles and is therefore much denser in the tip.

The most telling warning sign for the novice buyer is that the handle is centered in a paste or paintbrush and extends a little more than four inches, like a rod or thumb, out of the base. Handles on stipplers are usually bow- or J-shaped.

Stippler sizes range from 1″ × 4″ to 4″ × 6″. Don't bother with the smaller size. They are more cumbersome to handle since straight contact with the surface is difficult. The best approach to this technique is gentle transition of one color into another.

Materials

Negative

♦ glaze or thinned paint or paint thickened with whitening (chalk) or fine silica sand (if a three-dimensional texture is desired)

♦ stipple brush

Stippling, Negative

1 Effective negative stippling can best be executed with a glaze. If you are using paint, be certain to thin it unless you prefer a three-dimensional texture. For such effects, you can actually thicken a paint by adding whitening (chalk) or fine silica sand. The most obvious disadvantages to doing so are the reduction of adhesion and the fact that this type of texture will be difficult to reverse when redecorating.

First, apply the glaze. When using more than one color, be certain to blend them at least roughly. Stippling is a useful technique to achieve the finest, most delicate transitions from one color to another. Rough stippling will create a finer stipple texture.

2 To stipple, simply pounce the brush's bristle tips, making flat contact with the surface and leaving a fine bristle tip imprint in the wet glaze. First stipple gently and randomly, always making certain that the flat surface of the bristle tips make flat contact.

3 Then close the pattern and refine it to your taste or need.

4 Stipple until you create a fine sand texture.

Stippling, Positive

1 To create a coarser, almost sponging-on effect, apply thinned paint or glaze to the bristle tips—more for a rougher texture, less for a finer texture. In some cases, you may want to work some of the medium off on a rag or board prior to stippling your project area.

Materials

Positive

♦ glaze or thinned paint

♦ stipple brush

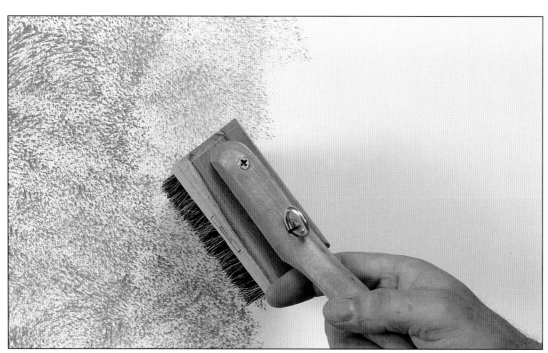

2 Pounce the stipple brush's bristle tips flat onto the surface, at first gently, then a little harder to create a suitable texture. An intense positive stipple can be executed to resemble the texture of its negative cousin.

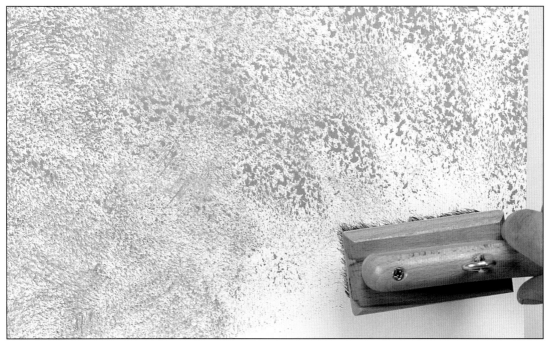

3 Two or more colors may be stippled together or in separate applications. They should overlap and fade into one another. Again, a drier brush will create a fainter, finer texture. Stippling into a wet base or combining positive and negative applications are alternatives.

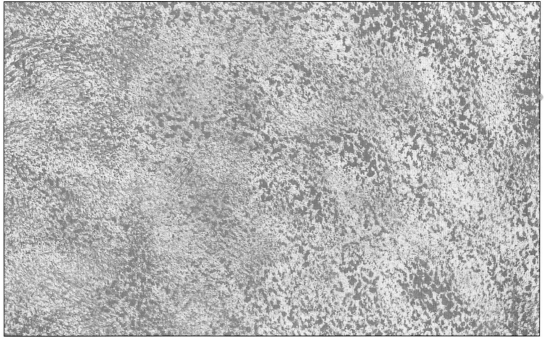

4 The finished texture will vary according to your mode of execution. If the texture is fine, it may resemble sandstone. When it is rough, it will imitate a dull granite or spongelike texture.

The heartgrainer or rocker is a basic graining tool available in several models and sizes. The name *heartgrainer* is appropriate since the effect this tool achieves is that of the heart of the wood's grain, but the tool is also known as a rocker or graining tool. It is usually used in partnership with various combs, mottlers and floggers. Rockers are made from plastic or rubber pulled over a wooden or plastic quarter-round shoe with or without a handle. The more expensive models are made of solid rubber. Rockers are available in a greater variety of widths and sizes of grain.

Look-Rite Faux Products has reintroduced rubber woodgraining tools in several different patterns and sizes. These versatile wood art tools are not mounted but are made to be wrapped around a cylinder, such as a can or PVC pipe. They are worthwhile purchases for both professional and amateur woodgrainers who enjoy working with rockers.

A variation of this tool is a graining roller, which is usually mounted on a wire frame. It works using the same principal as the rocker, but requires more practice to get a good result.

Choose the tool that is easiest for you to handle.

Using your chosen tool, apply a thin coat of glaze over a satin-sheen base. Lightly mottle or wipe the glaze with a soft cotton knit rag so that only a very thin film of the glaze remains. If you wipe the glaze, do so in the direction of the grain effect you wish to create. Pull the rocker through the glaze, slowly rocking its head as you press and pull it down. Pressure and movement must be continuous. The speed at which you move and rock the rocker determines the grain pattern. For greater variety, rock at infrequent intervals, changing the contact points and rocking motion. Practice and test the pressure you need to arrive at a good clean image. The head of most basic rockers can be reversed. Other models are simply turned over for greater variety.

To enhance this simple pattern, pull a comb straight through some of the vertical bands between the "heart" areas. You can strié the wood grain lightly with a flogger while the glaze is still tacky.

The effect achieved using the rocker can be quite stunning, but there are inherent limitations. The pattern created is often obvious and predictable. However, there is a country charm about it, especially when you are trying for a pine or oak look.

Materials

- thin glaze of Burnt Umber and Burnt Sienna
- base of light terra-cotta
- heartgrainer or rocker

As you gain experience, you can achieve more of an oak look by using a graduated comb to create side grains on both sides next to the heart grain. Pull the comb at a 45° angle through the glaze with the wider teeth toward the heart. You can also use steel combs to create a similar effect. While the glaze is still wet, lightly pull a triangular comb through the side grain at a slight angle toward the center, followed by a small, fine steel comb. Then take a check roller and bristle or foam brush with a small amount of glaze on it, lay the brush bristle or foam on top of the check roller, roll it up the heartgrain and then over the straight grain. This will give you a grain pore effect. With a dry mottler or flogger, whisk out the pores in a downward motion into longer, thinner streaks.

For more sophisticated woodgrain effects, hand-painting methods are used.

Heartgraining (Rocking)

1 Simple, successful imitations of heartgrain wood, similar to pine or oak, may be created by using one of the many available models of heartgrainer or rocker. Most of these rubber or plastic tools will work well, although the solid rubber varieties do make better surface contact. Apply a very thin coat of glaze, in this case mixed from Burnt Umber and Burnt Sienna, over a light terra-cotta base.

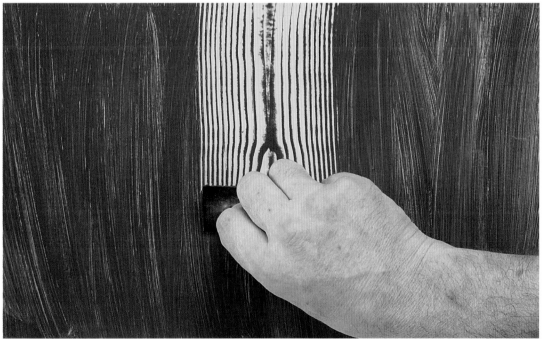

2 Pull the rocker in a steady motion through the glaze while applying constant downward pressure and rocking ever so slightly in one direction or back and forth. The first movement will give you an open heartgrain, the latter a closed heartgrain. Rockers may be reversed and the initial contact point may be anywhere on its grooved surface. Exercising these options will help you create diverse wood-grain effects.

3 As you work the rocker through the glaze, paint will collect in its grooves. Wipe these residues out periodically to ensure clean grain images. Add side grains by using of a regularly spaced or varied rubber comb. Although many rockers have a comb attachment, most of these are limited in use. Choose the proper width of teeth to match the heartgrain and extend the side grain off the heart. The teeth of rubber combs are usually pointed, concave or edged on one side. The sharpest edges should make contact with the surface. This ensures the best contact and medium displacement.

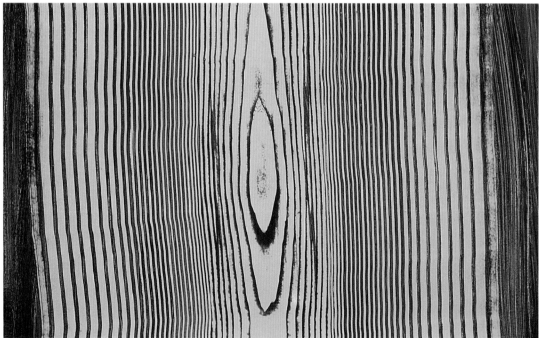

4 The finished grain should be a simple yet convincing facsimile of a piece of wood or a plank. The images may be embellished through flogging and overgraining.

To simulate a moiré (pro-nounced *mwar-ray*) effect, use the previously described heartgraining process, followed by lightly brushing horizontally across the grain with a flogger to create a woven look. Pastel colors are com-monly used in this technique.

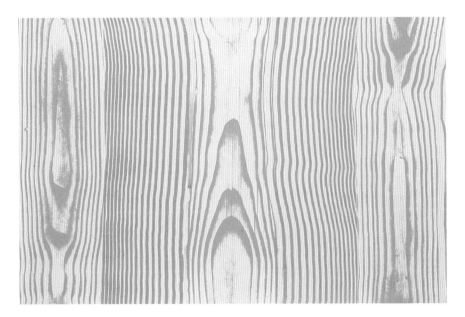

Moiré

1 The basis for this silk moiré effect is the same as for heartgraining. Your color selection should be suitable and common in such fabrics. Heartgrains should be alternated with straight grains running the length of the fabric.

 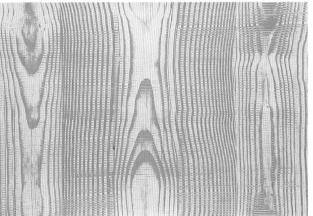

2 Complete the moiré effect by using a fine rubber graining comb. An even better tool is a flogging or dragging brush, which you pull through or drag over the still-wet and open glaze against the grain in only one direction.

3 The final effect should be discreet and delicate. For darker colors, consider using a medium deep base.

Originally, combing was a woodgraining method. It stands well on its own when used wisely. A regular or variegated rubber comb is pulled through the glaze or slightly thinned paint. Straight lines or herringbone patterns work best. Other designs are effective, but difficult to carry over a large surface. You can experiment by using one color for the base coat and a contrasting color for the glaze, and pulling the comb horizontally through the glaze the first time. Allow it to dry, apply the second color of glaze and then pull the comb through vertically.

Since this technique works best on smaller projects, you can cut your own comb from drawing board. The heavy cardboard tool will have a limited life expectancy. For a longer-lasting comb, use a section of vinyl baseboard. And for larger jobs, a suitable comb can be made from a window squeegee.

Materials

Squeegee

♦ commercial rubber or plastic faux finish comb, or handmade comb made from a window or shower squeegee that has been cut with a single-edge razor blade or utility knife

♦ colored glaze

♦ eggshell or satin-sheen base

♦ rag for wiping excess glaze from comb

Combing With Squeegee

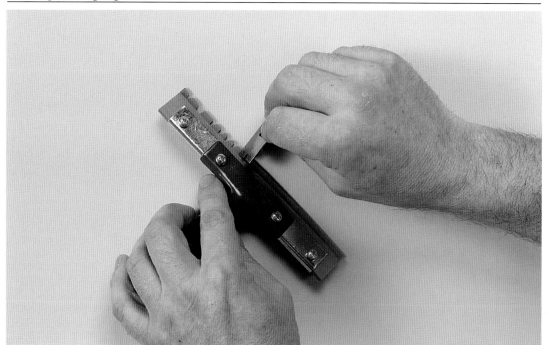

1 You don't have to purchase a commercially made rubber or plastic comb; you can make your own using any suitable material, even cardboard. The benefit is not so much economy as the ability to create a comb that suits your design needs best. For larger areas, you can turn a window or shower squeegee into a wonderful, practical tool. Using a single-edged razor blade or utility knife, cut out gaps to create teeth. In designing your pattern and cutting the comb, keep in mind that the teeth make contact with the surface and create negative lines.

2 Mix your color and add glazing liquid. Apply a thin, even coat of glaze over a dry eggshell or satin-sheen base color.

3 Pull your comb through the wet glaze at a slight angle with the teeth pointing down flat. Be sure to use adequate pressure to ensure a clear, clean image. After each pass, wipe the collected medium off the comb's teeth.

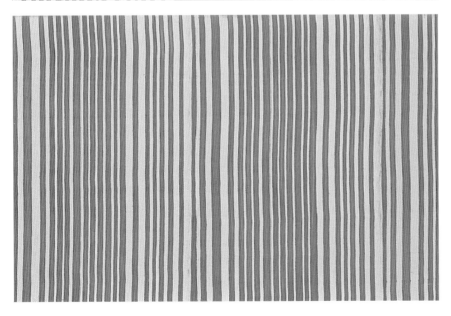

4 The lines should be as straight as possible. Since any comb can be custom designed and made to size, the finished texture may provide decorative options for frames as well as walls.

Combing With Overglaze

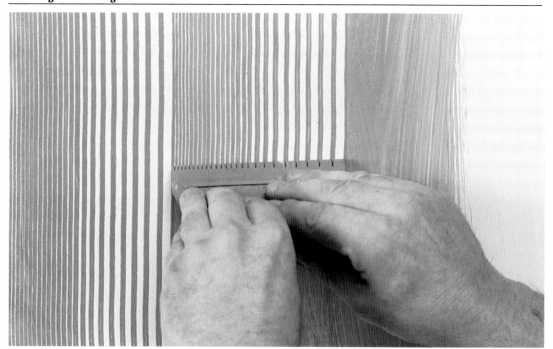

1 As before, apply a thin coat of glaze and comb vertically. When using a manufactured comb, such as the British-model variegated duplex, be sure that the sharp front edges of its teeth make contact through the glaze with the surface. Here a Mediterranean blue-green base was glazed over with Raw Sienna.

Materials

Overglaze

♦ two contrasting colors of glaze
♦ eggshell or satin-sheen base
♦ rubber comb

2 When the glaze is dry, overglaze by applying an even, thin coat of your choice of a similar or contrasting color of glaze. In this example, a deep purple was used. The final brush strokes should be in the opposite direction as in the first application (in this case, horizontal).

3 Now comb through the glaze in this horizontal direction. But first, consider whether you want to comb from the right to the left, or the opposite. This will determine whether the comb lines go from wide to fine, or vice versa. (If the direction is reversed with each pass, the comb lines will change gently from fine to wide and back to fine.)

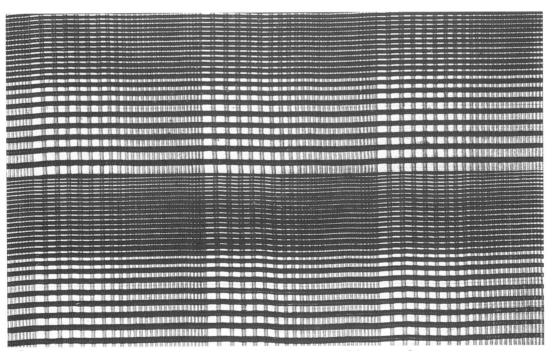

4 The finished product has a plaid quality. Although numerous possibilities exist for designing patterns and textures with the use of combs, the best ones are very simple. Only they will give you the guarantee of an easy, professional-looking execution.

Combing, One Color: Traditional, Herringbone, Abstract

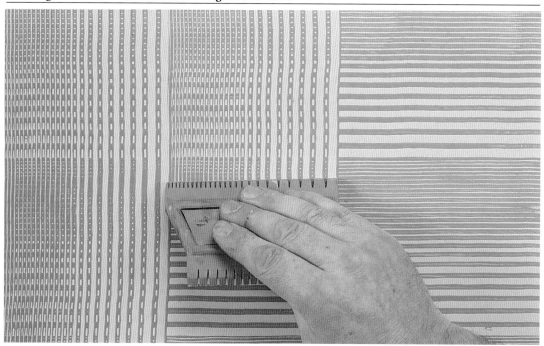

1 This technique also requires two combing passes, but both are done to the same coat of glaze while it is still wet. Apply a thin coat of glaze over the base coat. Comb vertically from top to bottom. Immediately comb across from right to left or vice versa.

One Color

♦ colored glaze
♦ eggshell or satin-sheen base
♦ rubber comb

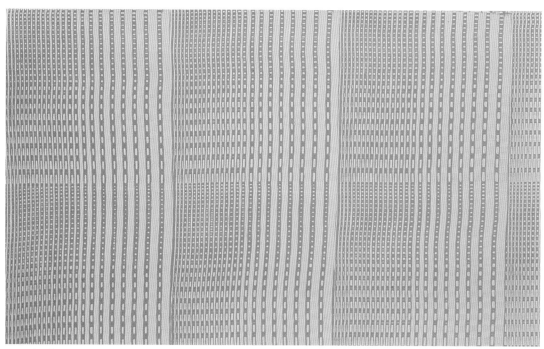

2 The finished texture is identical to that produced by combing with an overglaze, but uses only two colors and can be done in one step.

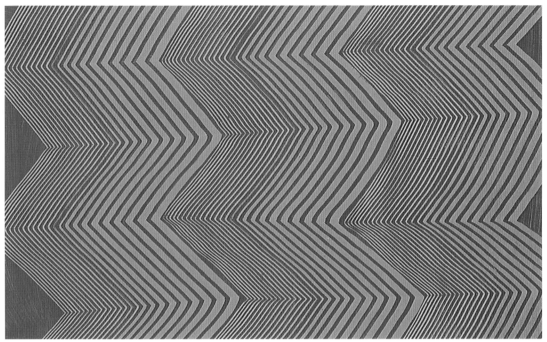

3 An attractive alternative is a herringbone pattern. Apply your glaze and comb through it in a zigzag motion. Try to repeat each pass as accurately as possible. This effect is difficult to execute on larger areas since the design has a tendency to drift.

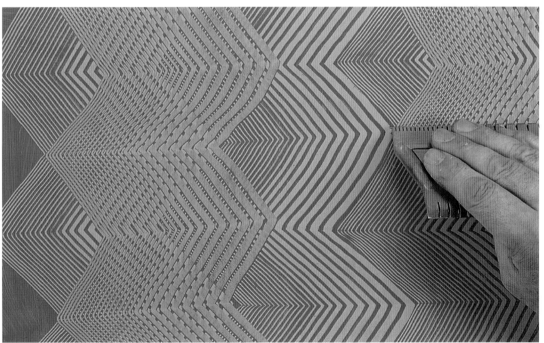

4 Again, we are faced with a multitude of alternatives. Here, a zigzag pattern is pulled in the opposite direction over the first. Also, one pattern is skipped. Play and invent to create your own pattern, or create a random, abstract design.

Time, nature and neglect are the best antiquers. Obviously, there are those who are unwilling to wait for natural decay to do its work. You may remember "antique" furnishings available in the sixties and seventies. They had been beaten with chains and barbed wire, or dragged for miles behind vehicles. I have witnessed harsh acid used to age fine handmade weapons, and crockery left in the swamp to "age" it more quickly. Any cultured or sensitive individual should object to "aging" methods that destroy pieces of art or fine furnishings in order to make a quick, easy buck.

If an item is damaged, repair, restore, and touch it up. If it is beyond these means, rebuild and repaint it. I think it is perfectly acceptable to paint a newly made object in a traditional style using old methods and materials, but it is not necessary to beat up or abuse your surface. Age and wear need not imply neglect.

Some years ago, a New York antique dealer brought a side table to my studio. The piece was not extremely old, maybe sixty or so years, but it had nice, classical lines. Someone had applied what appeared to be porch or deck paint and the veneer was lifting off. The only solution was to strip, repair and repaint it. When finished, the top was painted as a white and green Scandinavian marble. The rest of the table was painted in an ivory color with light green and salmon accents. The drawers were treated with a strié in a fawn color. Then the whole piece was lightly antiqued. It was a stunning piece . . .

until the dealer arrived. The dealer wanted more antiquing! I applied a deep Raw Umber glaze. . . . More! I sanded and stained the corners. . . . More! He demanded that I use bleach and acids to make the paint crack and peel.

Obviously, there are many ways to antique a surface. One way is by simply applying a thin coat of glaze. Umber can be used to tint the glaze and can then be brushed or wiped into the crevices. The glaze can also be tinted with a spot of white to resemble dust. You can try using a heavier, darker glaze and mottling or wiping it. Glaze the surface twice: First apply a lighter glaze, wipe lightly, and then apply a darker one and wipe thoroughly until it remains only in the nooks and crannies.

When antiquing, consider natural wear on corners, drawers and doors. Think about how and where the object would have been cleaned and by whom. Did Mimi dust off the top with a feather duster—or did Brunhilda regularly scrub it down during her weekly tirade?

New raw wood may be stained the color of old wood or basecoated and woodgrained for the same effect. In this case, you may want to seal the surface with an acrylic varnish/sealer or, even better, with an oil- or alkyd-based varnish or polyurethane.

Using latex paints, apply two or more coats of different traditional colors. Be sure to let each dry properly, perhaps even applying an antiquing layer over each coat. Latex and acrylics are soluble in denatured alcohol. Since alcohol evaporates

Materials

- three or more colors of paint
- glaze of Raw Umber
- denatured or rubbing alcohol
- oil-based polyurethane or shellac
- cotton knit rag

quickly, the wetter the area is kept, the easier it will be to remove the paint. Strategically "wash and wear" the surface to reveal consecutive coats of paint. Corners and edges may be "worn" down to the bare natural or faux wood. Follow by antiquing the project.

Antiquing

1 There are numerous processes you can use to create the appearance of antique or distressed surfaces with the aid of paint. Alcohol, in this case strong denatured or rubbing alcohol, will dissolve acrylic paints, so you can apply multiple layers of different-colored acrylic paint to your surface and reveal them with alcohol. Of course, each coat must dry reasonably well prior to painting over it.

The first coat of this example was a wood color. This may be sealed with an oil-based polyurethane or shellac to prevent the alcohol from penetrating through it. A natural stained wood will also provide an excellent base. The following coats were institutional green, white and blue.

2 When the paint is dry, saturate a cotton knit rag with alcohol and begin washing the area.

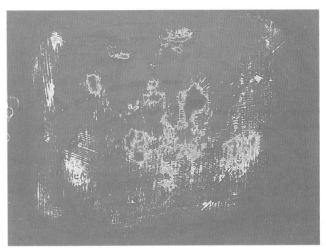

3 Begin to rub harder in strategic areas to start revealing the earlier coats. Alcohol evaporates rather quickly. Use it liberally and let it work for you. Ventilation is important since the odor of the alcohol is pungent and intoxicating.

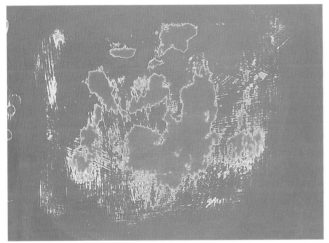

4 The finished texture will appear distressed and worn. When employing this technique on three-dimensional surfaces, such as furniture, concentrate your efforts on the areas that naturally and logically get worn—corners, edges and around handles and locks. Of course, you must not ignore adding general, overall wear to your "antique."

5 To further enhance the antique appearance of the surface, apply a transparent, thin coat of Raw Umber glaze. Raw Umber is best when muted with a hint of white so it has the appearance of dark dust.

6 Mottle the surface by dabbing over the glaze with a cotton knit rag, giving the surface a cloudy, dirty appearance.

7 Mottle over it again with a pounce-shaped rag ball to refine and soften the texture.

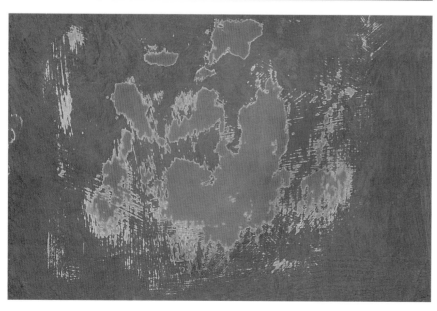

Antiquing Crown Molding

On three-dimensional surfaces, wipe over the raised areas that are subjected to normal wear. First wipe gently, then a little harder in strategic areas. Deeply recessed moldings may be overglazed with a slightly darker and heavier glaze. The glaze should be mottled and wiped hard to leave residue only in the deepest crevices. (Because I was working on such a small sample of crown molding, I set the sample on its side.)

Materials

Crown Molding

- ◆ eggshell or satin-sheen base
- ◆ glaze
- ◆ housepainting brush
- ◆ cotton knit rag
- ◆ flat white bristle brush
- ◆ masking tape
- ◆ brush

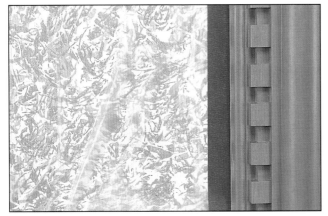

1 Prior to antiquing or highlighting a crown molding or other three-dimensional object, it needs to be prepared properly. Today's antiques were usually painted by highly skilled professionals. Your "antique" should have the same base. The best undercoat will be an eggshell or satin sheen. Tape off the molding and cover areas that require protection.

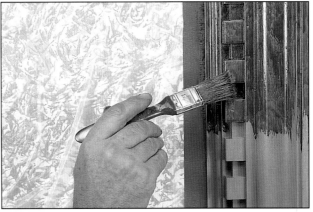

2 Apply a thin coat of glaze. In this case, Raw Umber with a hint of white was used. Brushing on the glaze is recommended. Be sure not to leave any "holidays"—missed spots in the tight corners and crevices. Those areas would logically display the most discoloration.

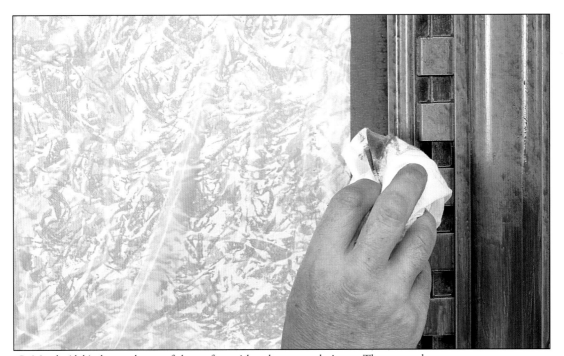

3 Mottle (dab) the top layers of the surface with a dry cotton knit rag. The rag works best when shaped into a pounce so it will not reach deep into the recessed areas. Ball up the rag but make sure it has a smooth outer layer and is somewhat flattened by hitting it in the palm of your hand.

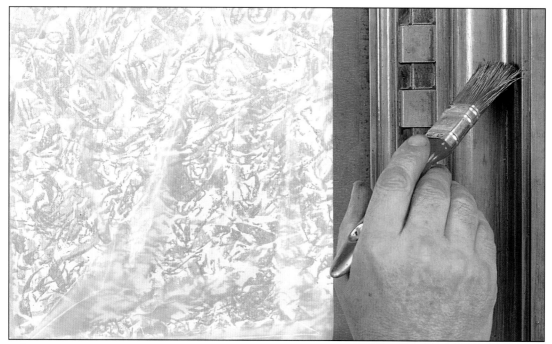

4 While the glaze is still a little open, drybrush the crevices to lightly tone these areas. This will help disperse, soften and feather out any excess glaze and create a gentler transition from the naturally darker, recessed areas into the lighter, raised images.

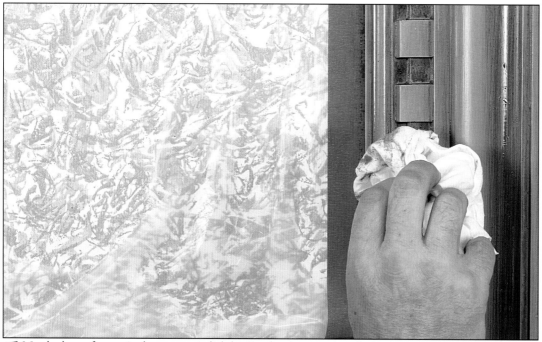

5 Mottle the surface again, but now very lightly. Gently wipe over the raised areas to further highlight them by almost completely ridding them of glaze.

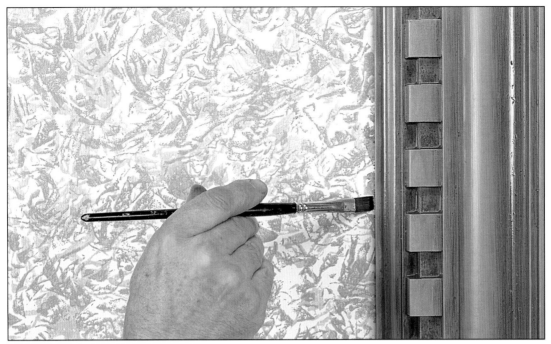

6 Carefully remove the masking tape behind you as you proceed. This is important.
Since glaze may have seeped under the tape and acrylics dry relatively quickly,
cleanup must be done as soon as possible. Using a clean, flat brush that has been dampened with water, loosen and remove any offending spots.

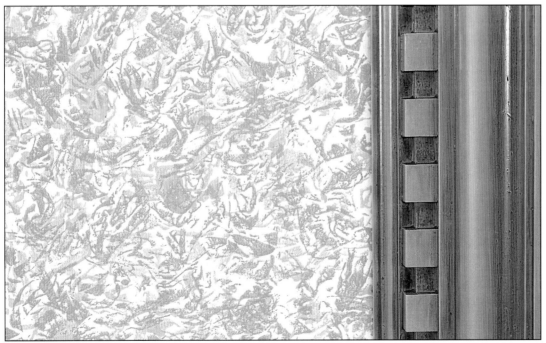

7 The finished product should have a believable, highlighted and low-lighted effect,
smart and not overstated. The wall treatment on this example is a positive rag-roll in
a Continental style.

While I was still an apprentice, I had several occasions to employ this technique to decorate the wainscoting in the stair halls of older tenement buildings in Berlin. The base coat was usually of a brilliant nature in colors such as yellow, orange, red and yellow green. The top coat was generally deep and warm. This is not to say that such combinations are necessarily beautiful, but they were effective and traditional for many of those types of buildings.

Today there are a variety of crackling products available in kits. If you find or hear of a product with promise, test it to check its suitability. Beware of lacquer-based products since generally they are not compatible with most other paints.

One method to create a clear cracked finish is to apply an oil-based polyurethane varnish over a dry latex base coat. Let it set (but not dry), then apply an *acrylic polyurethane varnish*. Rub the desired color in the cracks when dry.

Perhaps the most popular crackling technique today involves the use of hide glue. When purchasing such glue, check the expiration date on the container. Apply a base coat of latex. When it is dry, put on a coat of the hide glue. This glue is quite sticky and heavy-bodied. Although it can be applied straight, I suggest diluting two parts glue with up to one part water for easier application. The depth of the cracks are somewhat determined by the thickness of this coat of glue. When the glue feels dry, usually in one to three days,

apply a coat of the surface latex paint over the glue. Here is where difficulties may occur. Water will loosen and open the glue. Since the latex paint contains water, it will dissolve the glue immediately, eliminating any time to play with the coating. Therefore, brushing a larger area is especially difficult and requires planning and practice. The top coat will set up fast while the revitalized glue coat underneath will dry more slowly, cracking the top coat.

Since the glue now exposed to the elements by the cracks remains water soluble, you will need to apply one or two coats of a sealer or varnish—I recommend an oil-based polyurethane varnish. I also recommend priming all of the surfaces with two coats of nonacrylic paint to prevent moisture from reaching the glue from the inside.

During my last visit to Germany, I learned of another technique that creates a raised crackle effect. A low sheen or flat enamel is applied to the surface and allowed to dry, then sanded to dull the surface. Make a glaze of beer, vinegar or acrylic varnish, or simply use any acrylic glazing medium and apply it to the surface. When it is dry, apply a coat of clear, low-sheen or flat oil-based polyurethane varnish. While this coat is still uncured and somewhat tacky, apply a coat of dextrin. This is a starch-gum product found in powder form at a drug or grocery store. Dissolve enough of the powder in hot water to achieve a varnish consistency.

Apply this mixture to the uncured

- commercial crackling medium or hide glue
- flat acrylic house paint
- housepainting brush
- sealer

polyurethane surface using a paintbrush. This coat may be lightly stippled to create a more even surface. Be careful not to be too exuberant because the polyurethane undersurface needs to remain undisturbed.

Crackling occurs as the varnish rips apart due to the enormous tension created by the drying dextrin coat over the uncured polyurethane. This effect is similar to the hide glue, but is slower and more controllable. The pattern of the crackle is dependent upon the temperature of the surface as it dries. A lower temperature creates a finer crackle; a higher temperature creates a larger crackle. A hair dryer may be used to control the temperature and crackle pattern.

As soon as the crackle has finished developing and the dextrin is dry, apply an oil-based glaze or wax patina. Use a medium-dry glaze of a darker contrasting color, and work it into the cracks so that they are clearly visible.

After the glaze has set up, wash off the dextrin with a soft sponge and water. You must be extremely cautious not to wash out the glaze. If the glaze is disturbed, the area may be sanded gently with pumice powder when it is completely dry.

Finally, protect the surface with a minimum of one coat of varnish.

Crackling

1 Crackle finishing is a very popular antiquing and decorating method. Many manufacturers produce positive as well as negative crackling mediums. Most work on the basis of a slow-curing medium being covered by a fast-drying one. The hide glue method works when the glue base reopens, usually by absorbing water. Unfortunately, this type of finish is very vulnerable to weather conditions. When using the hide glue method, be sure that the glue is fresh. Hide glue has a shelf life of up to two years. Thin the glue with two to three parts of water. Apply an even coat over the dry base. The depth of the crackle is determined by the thickness of the glue.

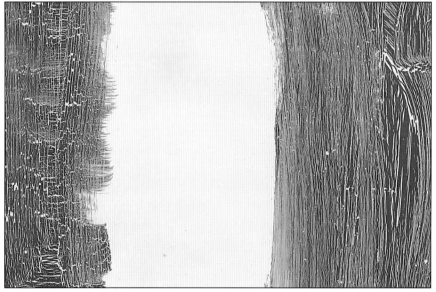

2 Permit the hide glue to dry for up to three days. Prepare a contrasting color of a flat acrylic house paint. Thin it slightly and apply it over the dry glue. The hide glue will absorb the moisture contents of the paint instantly. This forces the new coat of paint to dry rapidly, while the glue opens again, thus forcing the top layer to crack.

3 The natural process that prompts the formation of the cracks is also what makes this technique cumbersome and the finished work fragile. The fact that the glue opens instantly when subjected to moisture requires you to apply the top layer of acrylic quickly, decisively and without much brushing over the dry edges. The direction of the strokes will determine the flow of the cracks. It is advised to complete such finishes with a sealer that is not waterbased. Humidity and water will reactivate the glue.

Natural corrosion and oxidization affect all metals. On bronze, brass and copper, these processes create a patinated surface rich in color mostly in the green and blue families but containing hints of brown and white. You can replicate these processes on metal decorations, rough iron, tin ceilings, cornices, doors or any other surface.

Many gold-bronze paint products are available. LaScaux and other manufacturers make fine acrylic metal paints. Since the pigments in these paints are ground metal, the resulting finish is rather porous and it is best to seal it with a low-sheen poly or clear acrylic varnish.

Metal paints are made essentially the same way as any other. The pigment is finely ground metal powder, such as bronze, copper, brass and aluminum, but seldom gold or silver. Most people still refer to such paints as gold and silver even though these pigments are traditionally called bronzing powders. They are made in a variety of shades, including green, purple and other colored metallics. Quality products are most often found in art or silkscreen supply shops rather than in the average hobby outlet or catalog.

These paints can be bought premixed, or you can make your own by adding bronzing powder to a quality acrylic glazing medium or varnish. Again, you must find the balance between opaqueness and breakdown. You need to have decent coverage, but not at the cost of paint failure. If the mix is too dry, it may cause the paint to dissolve in the overglazing process. As is often the case, two thin coats may be better than one to create a proper base. If you believe the paint may break down but only slightly, you can "fix" the surface by misting it with a fixative or coating it with a low-sheen acrylic sealer.

When dry, apply a thin coat of a very liquid transparent glaze that has been tinted with Raw or Burnt Umber and a hint of Raw Sienna or Phthalo Green. Coat a section of the surface using a brush or sponge, thus letting water or alcohol flow through it. When this is not possible, such as on ceilings or ornate surfaces, wet it with clear glazing liquid and then wash colored glaze into strategic areas. This slightly tones the "metal" to reproduce natural oxidation through pollution or water staining. If the surface still feels a little tacky the following day, you should wait another day before proceeding.

Latex products are ideal because large amounts of liquid are needed to allow the verdigris colors to flow freely. Mix three to six verdigris colors (such as mint green, blue green or pale blue) in a latex paint. For a color that looks like swamp water, use a little white or off-white and some blue-green toned with Raw Umber. For that poisonous brilliance, mix in a little Phthalo Blue or Green. Thin portions of this paint for good flow, leaving the rest opaque. Wet a section, top to bottom, with plenty of water or a mixture of water and glazing liquid, then wash in some of the swamp water color, perhaps slightly toned with Burnt Umber for a water-stained effect. To achieve a natural effect, use a fitch and apply the diluted colors in random patches. Now apply some water, allowing it to flow through the layer of wet paint so it runs down the surface. For more distinct verdigris, apply more of the various colors, letting them run into the established flow. For more flow, direct the water with a fitch or flick water onto the surface. Let the more concentrated colors run off the top edge and appear out of joints and crevices. Do not wind up with a surface that is entirely painted in the verdigris colors. Let the "metal" shine through. Cover the floor, and let it rain!

When it is dry you may want to protect the surface by applying a coat of low-sheen poly or acrylic varnish.

A similar process gives a steel effect. Paint the surface with silver (aluminum) paint and seal it if necessary. Wet the surface down and let some rust-colored glaze run over the surface.

Materials

- metal paint
- sealer
- denatured or rubbing alcohol
- colored glaze
- three or more paints: Titanium White, Phthalo Green, Raw and Burnt Umber and Sienna
- brush

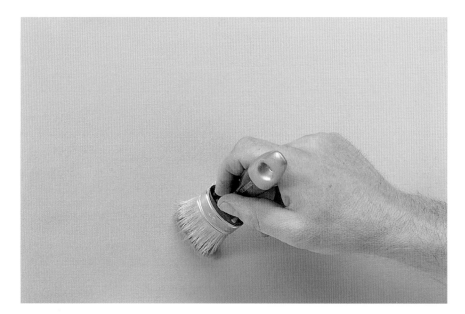

Verdigris

1 Imitations of oxidized metal are created over a base coated with a suitable metal paint. Such paints, often labeled gold or silver, are usually made of bronze, copper, brass or aluminum. Apply a coat of your choice of "gold" paint and let it dry.

2 Some gold paints are subject to oxidation. To prevent this, it may be advisable to use a sealer. To age the "metal," apply a thin Burnt Umber glaze over the dry gold surface.

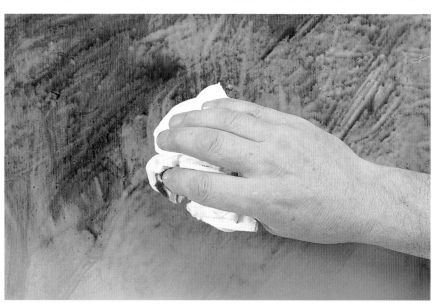

3 Mottle the glaze, first to texture the glaze, then to soften the effect. To begin creating the washed, weathered look, let water run from the top of the treated area down, allowing it to find its own path through the wet glaze. If the glaze is too set up, use denatured or rubbing alcohol. If the alcohol is too potent and dramatic, you may thin it with water. Testing the process on a practice board is always recommended.

4 Let the glaze dry. Prepare several colors ranging from white to Phthalo Green and Raw Umber. Also mix several color combinations out of these basic colors. Thin all colors in various degrees, wet the surface, and let these thinned paints run down over the antiqued gold.

5 Help the flowing process by strategically adding water as you proceed. This can be done with a brush or by spritzing (flicking or spraying) more general areas. Be sure to make it appear that these colors ran naturally.

6 Highlight the effect by creating a logical buildup of pigments that flow from the top down, thus creating the typical verdigris trails of multicolor accents—Phthalo Greens accented and toned by white, as well as hints of Raw Umber.

7 The finished product may appear subdued or dramatic. Do not overdo a good thing. Depending on the "age" you wish to create—ancient or simply antique—be certain that the surface reveals enough metal to make it realistic. (Logical buildup of oxidation is on the top edges. Then these pigmentations are washed downward, some settling on bottom edges or ledges.)

Part 3

ELEGANT FAUX FINISH TECHNIQUES

When you look at marble, you see the polished surface. But to understand the stone better, we must remember that it is three-dimensional. Do not only consider the surface, but also what lies underneath it and what it once was. Some, such as breccia, appear like molten lava with broken chunks of crusted ashes flowing within it. Others have veins that look like the roots of a tree that appear and disappear, dissolving like colored streams of liquid into sand. Others have veins that wiggle, twist and coil, or ones that run straight, bold and sharp.

FEATHER VEINING

A goose flight-wing tip or primary feather remains the ideal tool for faux veining. Other feathers that work are swan, duck, crow, lark, dove, sparrow or chicken. Turkey feathers are readily available and commonly sold as faux marble tools, but they are usually too soft and so are not suitable for marbling. The barbules (barbs extending from the shaft of the feather) do not have the ideal spring or resilience for the job.

A goose feather is definitely your best choice. View the feather as a brush: the barbules are the hairs and shaft, and the quill is the handle, which is both wide and narrow. The paint flows along the front and back of the goose feather, not along the top or bottom of the barbules. Although both sides of the feather may be used, the back (the side with the longer barbs that the tip curves toward) provides the best flow even though the front may give you a finer vein. By using the side of the tip you can make extremely fine lines. A delicate touch and steady hand are required to imitate what nature does casually.

Dip the tip of the feather into the media. On the edge of the container, wipe the excess paint or glaze off the flat side of the feather in the direction of the barbs. Lightly pull the edge of the feather over the surface to create a fine vein. If equal pressure is used, the result will be a thin and even line. With a little more pressure, the vein can be made wider. Expand it by moving the feather sideways. Changes in the direction of a vein should be initiated from the quill.

Your early attempts at veining may be frustrating. Few people have immediate satisfactory results using this new and unusual tool. Veining requires practice. To achieve fine veins, practice using slight, continuous contact while pulling a long line with the very tip of the barbules. You can do this on a dry, set-up or wet mottled board as well as on surfaces dampened with glazing liquid. As a novice, consider delaying the veining on a project until after the surface is dry. This way it can be removed as many times as necessary until you are pleased with the results. Have a few feathers on hand and, no matter how frustrating the previous effort was, find a quiet moment to try again.

Other considerations when veining

To ensure the flow of the medium you may need to thin it to a workable consistency. If you want a more

Materials

- goose feather (can also be swan, duck, crow or lark) or traditional dagger or sword striper brush

opaque paint, add tinting pigments such as universal colorants. The medium used for veining can also be a glaze if you desire transparency.

Negative veins may also be pulled or washed into a wet glaze using a clean feather dampened with thinner or glazing liquid. Obviously, the reaction to water or alcohol will be more radical than to glazing liquid, so be cautious. Have the feather damp, not wet, and remember that the reaction is delayed. Play. Practice veining under all possible conditions on various practice boards to learn what will happen if. . . .

Veining

The best veining tool is also the most natural: a primary flight-wing tip feather from a goose. The best alternatives are the types of feathers used in making quill brushes—swan, duck, crow and lark. Of course, in an emergency, even a good sparrow or parrot feather may do. (Turkey feathers, on the other hand, are totally useless.) The most useful part of the feather is the front tip, so when selecting a feather, be certain that this tip is refined and in prime condition.

OTHER VEINING METHODS

If you are frustrated by "feather work" and looking for an alternative, try the sword or dagger striper. These brushes are used much like a feather: The tip makes contact with the surface and creates the fine lines. Added pressure makes a wider vein. You can also create a wider vein by rolling the brush handle between your fingers and moving it sideways.

For simple, folk art-type veins, any artist brush will do: filbert, liner, round or flat. A wipe-out tool, the edge of cardboard, leather, rubber erasers and oil pastels may be employed as allies in veining.

Some images that are integrated in nature stand out like the proverbial sore thumb when brought inside for our uses. Nature may do it, but you, the faux finisher, may not. The most glaring of these no-nos are "bird's feet" or "spider webs" that are created when three or more veins join into one or when three or more lines intersect. Avoid rigid, uniform veining over an area.

For easier use and transportation, a feather may be shortened. About a three-inch section of the tip will do 95 percent of the work. Stripping the barbules off the base of this tip will furnish you with an exquisite little handle. Positive veins are created by loading the tip of a feather with medium and applying it into a wet or over a dry base. Negative veins are created when medium is removed from an open surface with a wet or dry feather. When doing this, be sure to compensate for any sideways curve in the feather. A little extra downward pressure or sideways movements will widen the vein.

The best substitute for a goose feather is a traditional dagger or sword striper brush. "Traditional" must be stressed here since some "modern" versions fall—literally—short of their mark. A striper's hair should be Blue or Kasan squirrel and from ferrule to tip should measure 1¾ to 2 inches long. The head of the brush is wide to carry a big load, flaring out into a hair-thin tip. Sizes range from no. 0 to no. 6. Overall length, including the short handle, is about 4½ inches.

Bad Veining

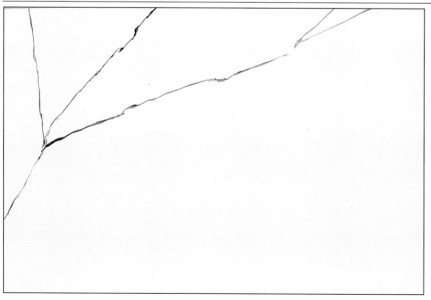

Veining requires practice. An "unfortunate" vein is not improved by adding an ugly one. Yet one well-executed, natural-looking vein is often all that is required to finish a simple, basic marble effect. "Bad" vein combinations include the "bird foot" where one vein branches into three at the same point.

This is another example of bad veining. Here three or more veins intersect at the same spot. It appears that a magnet is built into any crossing that pulls a following vein toward itself. It may help to visualize the placement of veins prior to pulling them. Do this by using a brush handle and holding it over the surface. Thus you can try different possible vein positions prior to actually making them permanent.

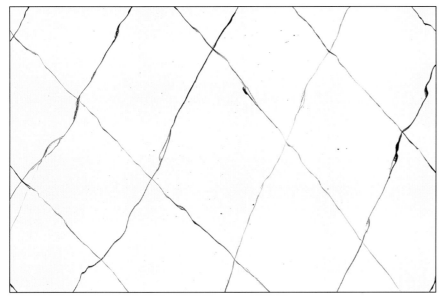

Another sample of bad veining is a regimental arrangment of lines. Here the placement of veins gives the appearance of a checkerboard or tic-tac-toe base. No matter how well-executed each individual vein may be, all efforts are in vain, so to speak, if you do not loosen up a little. There are many types of marbles; explore them in malls, tile shops, books, or your state or county capitol. Find some with simple, clear veins and learn to copy them.

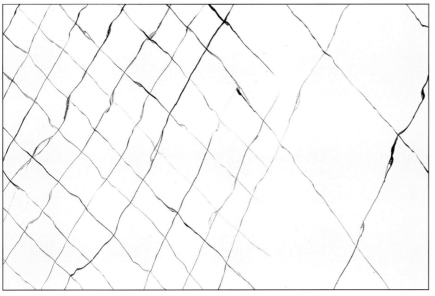

*B*ravura and fantasy faux marbles can be as simple as blending two or three colors, and may or may not include veining. These techniques may display a folk-art quality but also a simple, delightful sophistication.

Some of these techniques found application in woodworking and paneling, and more often in decorating armoires, cupboards and wardrobes. Here, marbling was commonly used on the cornice and molding, and, to a lesser degree, on the bases of the drawers.

Other than in folk woodgraining, glazes were rarely used in such basic marbling techniques. Generally, two or three colors were blended together at their edges to create a marbled look. Traditional color combinations include: dirty pink with a gold-green; white, gold, blue-gray and black; Raw Sienna, Burnt Sienna and white; and shades of powder blue, blue-gray and white.

Veins are usually painted into or over this surface with a small round artist's brush, which may be double-loaded (with black and white, for example).

You'll notice that some of these techniques call for the use of a pure badger softener. The purpose of the softener is to create an extremely delicate dispersion of an already fine texture. Too much softening creates a blended effect and general loss of design details. A blender, even one made from pure badger hair or even finer goat hair, will not be a suitable substitute. To use a well-designed pure badger softener, hold it at the low quarter of its handle (the handle is generally heavier toward the middle and top for counterbalance) with the hair tips of the flat brush point-ing straight down. Move the brush in long strokes over the wet surface, the tip barely touching the surface. If there is a defined grain, first go with the texture, then against it. Place the strokes side by side, then repeat if needed, perhaps in different directions. Placement depends on the texture or amount of blended effect you desire.

Materials

Bravura Marble

- satin-sheen white base
- light- to medium-colored paint or glaze
- clear glazing liquid
- denatured or rubbing alcohol
- brush
- natural sea sponge
- rag or paper towel
- goose feather or striper

Bravura Marble

1 Even the most basic marble effect can easily be enhanced by simple procedures. To create a quartzlike glaze undertone, little work and effort is required beyond the application of the base coat.

2 Immediately after applying a satinsheen white base coat and while it is still wet, use a brush and fold or blend in a light- to medium-colored blue or blue-gray paint or glaze in strategic areas.

3 Soften these areas, especially the edges, by blending the blue into the white. This is best accomplished when using the same brush. The brush should be relatively dry and without excessive pigments. If necessary, wipe the bristles off on a dry rag or paper towel.

4 The finished base's effect should be marblelike with discreet, soft contrast. Let dry.

5 Mix two colors—one, a dirty pink; the other, a medium gray. Turn a portion of each into a very transparent glaze by adding glazing liquid. Apply a moderate coat of clear glazing liquid to the painting surface and begin sponging in the pink glaze.

6 The sponged texture should appear random, but nevertheless planned and strategic. Again, create a rough but marblish effect. Now sponge in the gray colored glaze, being sure not to permit this color to dominate.

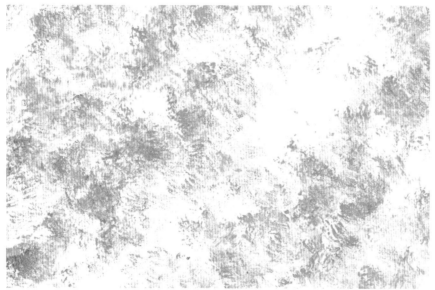

7 The intermediate effect should be rough-textured throughout. Its flow should conform with the flow of the texture underneath to establish a certain harmony.

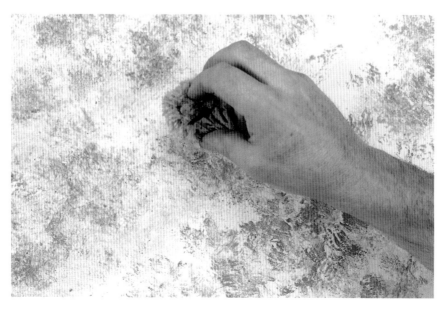

8 To soften the image, use a clean, natural sea sponge to sponge in a 50/50 glazing liquid-water mix to break up the dominating sponge textures.

9 To further break up these textures, especially the harder edges, use denatured or rubbing alcohol. Alcohol dissolves acrylics. Be sure to only dampen the sponge. Sponge in the alcohol, then lift it out, thus dispersing the texture.

10 While the glazes are still open, sponge in a little more of the colored glazes or the paint that was set aside from the original mixture. If these colors become too dominating, soften them too by wet sponging the area with clear glaze or alcohol.

11 Again, the finished sample should appear like generic marble.

12 For negative veining, use a primary goose feather or striper. Dampen or submerge it in alcohol, then dry it off slightly. Pull the vein. The alcohol's reaction depends on the dryness of the surface. It may be delayed. If so, immediately pull the vein again. The first stroke will apply the alcohol, the second will remove the dissolving medium.

13 This should be followed by pulling positive veins. For this you can use the original paints or glazes, depending on how opaque or transparent you want the veins to be. You may, of course, also use white and the other colors used in the original mixing: Raw Umber and Burnt Sienna.

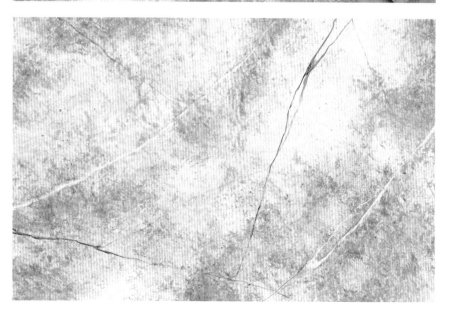

14 Basic veins are best when in harmony with the background treatment. They should integrate well into the flow and texture of the marble. A few minor veins can, and should, go against it. Visualize vein placement by holding a brush handle or pencil over the surface.

Bravura Mahogany

1 For most woodgraining effects, a variety of graining tools and brushes are employed. Most important among them are the mottler, flogger and softener brushes. However, common household materials may be used to create wonderful imitation effects—a six-inch section of a paint stir paddle and a cotton knit rag, for example. Score the stick on both sides with a single-edge razor blade or utility knife. Break the stick clear. This is your primary tool.

2 The secondary tool is a cotton knit rag of T-shirt stock. Carefully check an eight-inch square section to determine which side is the front. There is an inside and outside to any rag. Here the outside resembles a corduroy pattern, the other a weave. If you cannot discern the difference, use a printed shirt with the design on the outside.

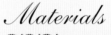

Materials

Bravura Mahogany

- three- to four-inch section of a paint stirring stick
- several cotton knit rags
- pure badger softening brush (if available)
- two separate glazes of Burnt Sienna and Burnt Umber

3 Double up the rag with the outside out and fold it over the length of the stick. The corduroy lines should run exactly parallel with the edge. Fold the remaining cloth over the ends, being certain to have control over the rag without stretching it. When using this tool, the folds must be away from the glaze. The smooth edge makes the contact with the surface.

4 Mix two separate glazes from Burnt Sienna and Burnt Umber. Mix more of the first since it must cover a far greater area. Apply a generous coat of the Burnt Sienna over most of the surface, except for the lower center section.

5 Paint what is to be the crotch area in the Burnt Umber glaze. Blend it at the perimeter with the surrounding Burnt Sienna for a fine transition of colors.

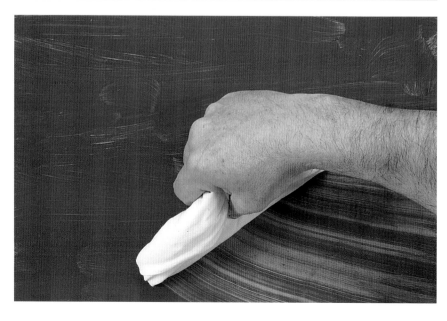

6 Place the rag-covered graining tool's edge lengthwise onto the corner or bottom edge of the surface. If you're right-handed, start from the left; if left-handed, start from the right. Be sure to place the inside corner just outside the center of the crotch area. Move the tool upward through the glaze.

7 As you move up toward the top, narrow the angle while concentrating on the inner edge of the tool. Leave untextured a fingerlike center image of the darker Burnt Umber.

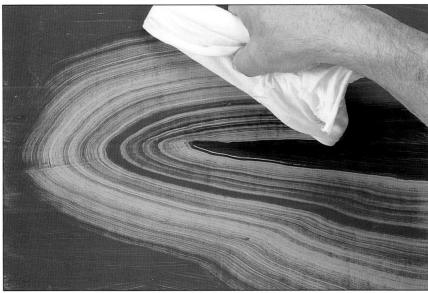

8 Although you must concentrate your attention on the inner edge, most movement is on the outer end of the graining tool. Movement should be continuous, narrowing the image as you move up and around an imaginary pivot.

9 The created image should be elegant, sweeping high with a continuous grain. The crotch area is dark and from it the defined grain extends in colors ranging from Burnt Umber to Burnt Sienna.

10 Use a smaller section of stirring paddle, about three to four inches long, to extend the grain into the remaining areas. Place the tool slightly inside the existing grain to avoid a build-up line, and follow the previously established grain pattern precisely.

11 Carefully mottle the dark center with a small section of a cotton knit rag. Be cautious not to disturb the grain surrounding the crotch area.

12 You can soften the finished product with a pure badger softening brush. First, soften the crotch area downward so as to not streak the dark color into the fine grain areas. Then soften very gently with the grain, then against it.

13 To plan the woodgrainer's movement, imagine a brush handle or finger covering the center of the Burnt Umber area. Move the graining tool around it in a sweeping motion.

"Bad" Bravura Mahogany

1 If the movement is not sweeping and narrowing toward the top, a boring, too regular arch is formed—certainly not a good wood imitation.

2 If the pivot is not *below* the inner edge of the board but *on* it, an equally offensive image is produced.

3 An incorrect pivot point produces an overlapping texture resembling a fan.

Bravura Burl

From the woodgrainer's perspective, bur or burl wood of any variety reigns among the most exquisite and challenging textures. The most realistic imitations will require, besides a fair amount of talent and experience, some fine tools and materials, such as a pure badger soft-ener, flogger, mottler, pencil and over-grainer. Bravura techniques often rely on tricks rather than specialized tools. Such makeshift "tools" enable us to create delightful images that, even if not true to nature, often capture the very essence of a texture.

Materials

Bravura Burl

- pure badger softener (if available)
- flogger
- mottler
- wavy mottler
- pencil overgrainer or finger brush
- light terra-cotta base
- three separate glazes of Raw Sienna, Burnt Sienna and Burnt Umber
- cotton knit rag
- small burler or fabric brush
- small, flat white bristle brush
- masking tape
- water, or denatured or rubbing alcohol

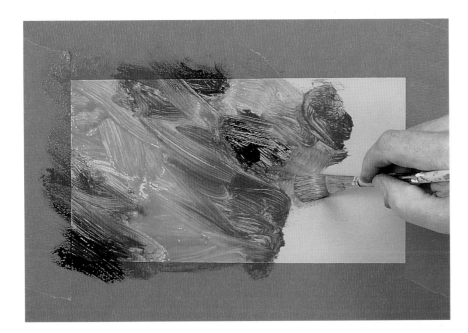

1 Make three glazes from Raw Sienna, Burnt Sienna and Burnt Umber. Apply generous amounts of each in rather organic shapes over a light terra-cotta base. Blend these colors where they meet to create variable shades and a better transition of colors.

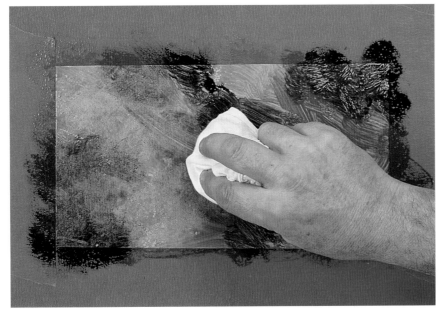

2 Mottle lightly to create the first texture and to disguise most brush marks, using a clean cotton knit rag. Be certain not to overwork and remove too much product. Leaving some glaze will help ensure enough open time for the procedures yet to come.

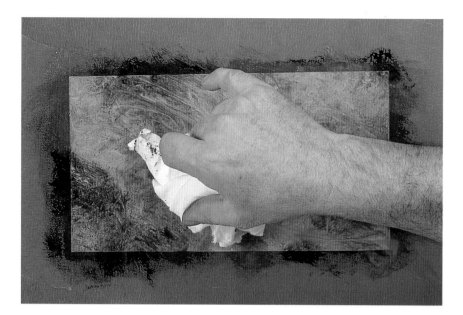

3 Lift the rag by its center, much like what was customary for fine ladies and gents in the days of powdered wigs. Now let the ends of the rag dance over the glaze—not like Brunhilda who works downstairs, but like Mimi, the upstairs maid. Dance the waltz and let the rag ends create a fine, random texture.

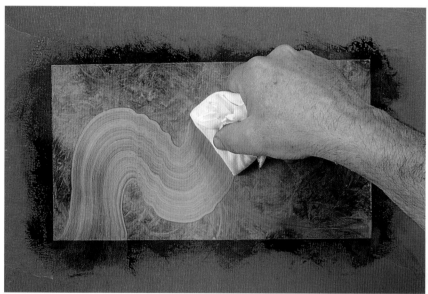

4 Fold the cotton knit rag over a paint stick as described in the project on mahogany. This time you should use two or three sizes ranging from one-and-a-half to three inches in length. Move your graining implement in a snakelike manner through the glaze.

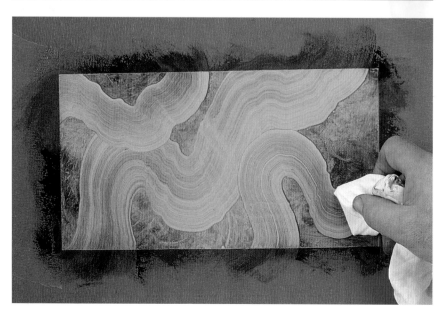

5 Don't imitate the movements of a tired snake, but of one that is on a caffeine or sugar high—maybe even a bit spastic. Alternate the stick sizes as you add images, leaving interesting negative areas untouched. Grain trails may appear to run into and over a previous image.

6 Now, while the glaze is still open, add the burs. Although these are naturally darker and located in the deeper shaded areas, in this bravura technique, place them throughout. Use a small burler or fabric brush and hold it by the very end of the handle. Place the tip of the bristle straight down onto the surface and twirl the brush between your fingertips.

7 In this bravura technique it is not necessary to add colors in the burling process. Use those colors already on the surface, transferring medium glaze to light areas, dark to medium and so on. The finished product should display a gentle quality with diverse textures that complement each other. Interesting negative areas with evidence of mottling and rag dancing must remain as a contrasting texture. Burs can be isolated or grouped in other areas.

8 If you are fortunate enough to own a pure badger softener (not to be mistaken with a blender) soften the surface very lightly. Remove the masking tape and clean the miters where medium may have seeped under the tape. This is best accomplished with the aid of a small, flat brush. Dampen the brush with water. Move the bristle's flat tip down along the edge of the miter to remove offensive spots. If the medium is too set up, carefully use alcohol.

Straightgraining

Straightgraining

- two separate glazes of Burnt Sienna and Burnt Umber
- light terra-cotta base
- small, flat white bristle brush (e.g., a mottler brush) or the rag and stick tool used for the bravura mahogany technique
- masking tape
- pure badger softener
- varnish or sealer

1 Straightgraining techniques are important in wood imitations. They are usually also very simple. As usual, such grains may be enhanced by overgraining as well as by undergraining with perhaps a flogging technique underneath. To illustrate the ease of this concept, apply a Burnt Sienna and Burnt Umber glaze onto a light terra-cotta base. Blend the colors where they meet.

2 Use a clean, dry white bristle brush. (A heavy white bristle mottler is the tool of choice. A well-made, better-quality white bristle artist or housepainting brush would be a good substitute.) Drag the tips of the bristles through the medium, creating a realistic, straight wood-grain effect. While a mottler brush is usually employed for this purpose, here too you can use the stick and rag method.

3 Prior to placing tape on a fragile, not yet cured finish, consider sealing the surface. In most cases, adding lint to the masking tape will prevent it from sticking too well. Tape off the miters of the first set of opposite areas. When taping off miters, be sure not to overprotect them. Let a fine hairline of the previously finished section show along the tape's edge. This line will enhance and better distinguish the miter.

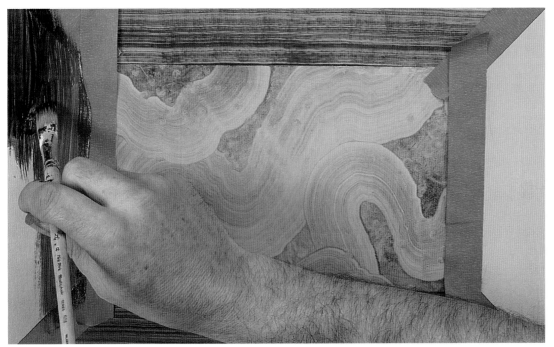

4 Score the tape's edge by pressing down with your thumb or, even better, your finger-nail. This will help seal the tape. Apply your glaze—in this case, two separate colors, Burnt Sienna and Burnt Umber—over the base. Be sure to blend well where the colors meet. Also be certain that glaze is applied throughout, including the tape edges. Pull your graining tool up through the glaze. Then pull the tape and clean all of the miters.

5 When your first application has properly dried, tape off the remaining sections, using caution and care in all proceedings. Apply your glazes and wood grain by pulling your cotton knit rag-covered stick straight through the glaze. If you wish to create a little extra texture, such as the appearance of light reflections, experiment by pulling your graining tool straight through the glaze, stopping it for a brief instant, then proceeding without lifting it off of the surface.

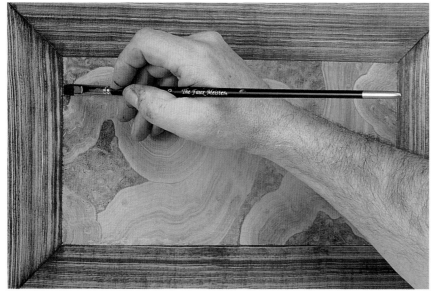

6 Softening the texture with a pure badger softener will improve the effect and make it more realistic. First, soften lightly in the direction of the grain, then against it. Remove the masking tape and clean the miters. All cautions apply if the previously textured areas were not sealed. Do not use alcohol in this case, as it will dissolve even cured acrylics. Even when using water, use caution.

7 The finished surface should be left to cure, or at least to dry well. Varnish or seal several times. If sanding is desired or necessary, be sure not to hasten to do so. Even after several coats of scaler, the protective coating is extremely thin. It is quickly sanded through, which would damage the delicate glaze underneath.

*M*arble is limestone changed through pressure and heat into a hard, crystalline stone. White marble is almost pure calcium carbonate, but most marbles show "impurities" of iron, magnesium, graphite and other substances. Because of these impurities, marble may be gray, brown, black and, in our case, green.

Verdé marble comes from all regions of the world, but mostly from Italy (hence the term *verdé*, which is Italian for green). It is amazing how many verdé marbles are available not only from Italy, but from other regions as far away as China and Brazil. Most verdé may be recognized by its lively dark-green color, which is mixed with black and interwoven with stark white. In some samples, you can also find nuances of other colors, mainly lavender and blue-green. Other species are rather pastel, or gray-green and yellow-green, and often highly contrasted with what appears to be black. The names

of some of these marbles are derived from their area of mining, for example, verdé di Genova. Others describe certain characteristics, for example verdé Antico, verdé Olivo or verdé Jaspe. Each type of marble may also have subspecies or varieties, such as dark, pale and breccia.

To make matters even more complicated (or, for faux finishers, more interesting), the marble may look similar yet still surprisingly unfamiliar depending on the specific section of the mountain where the marble is cut and how it is sliced. So while some pieces of marble may be well matched, select pieces and sections may be excitingly different.

Some of my favorite verde marbles are verdé Acceglio, verdé San Denise, verdé Giada, verdé Tinos and verdé Larissa. These are some of the more exciting varieties, displaying dramatic white veins and unique color accents. Imitating these marbles well can be quite challenging and requires at least some innovation, skill

Materials

- eggshell or satin-sheen white base
- clear glazing medium
- two different colors of glaze mixed from Mars Black, Phthalo Green and Titanium White
- plastic wrap
- goose feather or striper
- denatured or rubbing alcohol
- clean, dry cloth

and experience, not to mention patience and the proper tools. Most will require a minimum of one overglaze; others perhaps five. Color mixing and veining skills are also an important advantage.

Here, however, we'll explore the possibilities using a bravura technique, essentially frottage, to create very realistic marble imitations. Of course, this type of faux finish may be the basis of many other colored marbles.

Verdé

1 Since there are many varieties of verdé (green) marble, there are an equal number of approaches to its imitation. One of the easiest to execute is a form of frotting. A dry eggshell or satin-sheen white base is coated with a clear glazing medium made of about 40 percent retarder or extender, 60 percent glazing liquid and a dash of water.

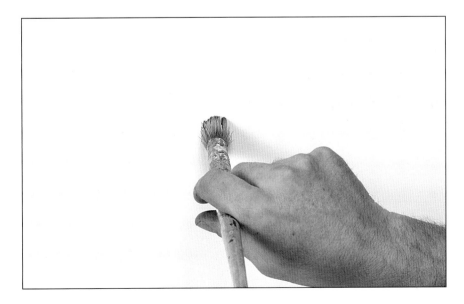

2 Mix two colors: 1) about five parts Ivory Black and one part Phthalo Green; 2) about ten parts Ivory Black to one part Phthalo green. Add perhaps 10 percent glazing medium to each. Fold and blend both colors into the clear glazing medium on the surface.

3 Apply each glaze to general areas or give them a marblelike flow, blending both with each other and the wet base. Some areas may occasionally have a stronger pigment. More clear glazing medium can be added to make these more transparent.

4 Lay plastic wrap onto the wet, glazed surface. The thinner, cheaper plastic is preferred since it permits a more active and interesting texture. Remove the plastic to reveal a marblelike texture.

5 Reverse the plastic and repeat the process by letting the plastic fall, this time in flowing folds, onto the surface. Tuck slightly on one end to create vein textures.

6 To break up some of the denser areas, use crumpled up plastic and dab it lightly into the glaze, being careful not to overdo a good thing. The finished product should be active, yet harmonious.

7 Bold quartz veins can be added with a goose feather or striper and alcohol. Since alcohol dissolves acrylics, it should be used sparingly in this technique. Dip the back edge of a feather in the alcohol, then remove any excess alcohol with a clean, dry cloth. Now apply the feather to the surface, thereby removing the medium and creating a vein.

8 Finer, negative veins are created in the same manner with the fine front tip of the feather. Here you must be sure that only a hint of solvent is used. Some frotted veinlike images may be extended so the look is more complete.

9 Now you may want to add some dark green and black veins. Most harmonious are those that run in the direction of the general flow of the whole texture. However, one vein or a few minor veins may run against the stream.

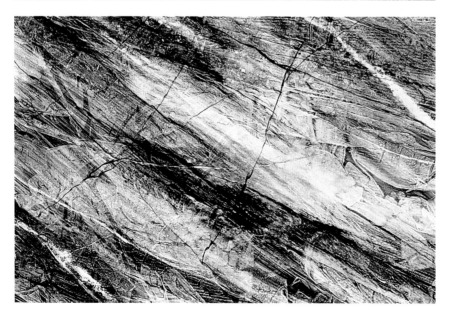

10 The finished texture should be active, yet harmonious. It's best when given the illusion of depth and transparency.

Verdé With Overglaze

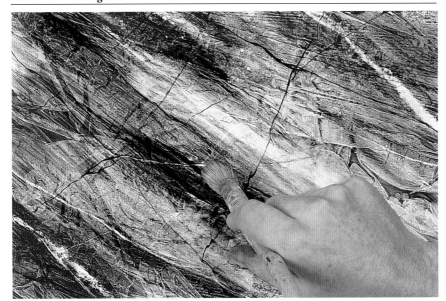

Materials

Overglaze

- eggshell or satin-sheen white base
- clear glazing medium
- two different colors of glaze mixed from Mars Black, Phthalo Green and Titanium White
- plastic wrap
- goose feather or striper
- denatured or rubbing alcohol
- clean, dry cloth

1 Faux verdé, like other marble and wood imitations, may be enhanced by overglazing. In this fashion, areas can be toned up or down as well as highlighted and otherwise embellished. Let the surface of the previously executed verdé dry and then apply a fresh coat of clear glazing medium.

2 Again, fold in your colored glazes, which should now be more transparent, ensuring that the previous work is enhanced, not eliminated. They may also be a little darker. Tone areas strategically and with purpose. Do not merely apply a coat of glaze over the entire surface; sculpt, build depth and add highlights to the texture. Again, add extra clear glazing medium in areas you wish to keep light.

3 Use the plastic wrap to lift out the glaze.

4 Add and highlight veins. Additional white veins may be added in the positive application of thinned white paint or glaze.

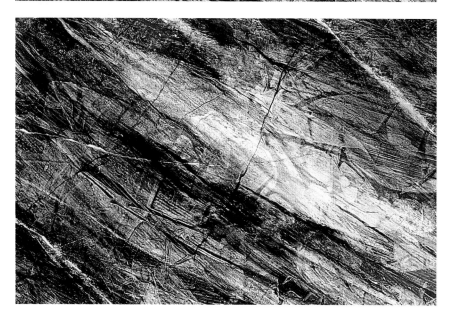

5 The overglazing process may be repeated in its entirety or on specific sections. Mottling and sponging, positive as well as negative, can also enhance the effect.

Few wood or marble imitations elicit as many expressions of delight and recognition as that of malachite. Some dictionaries will inform you that malachite is a dark emerald green basic carbonate of copper. Quite true, but more precisely, malachite is a stalagmitic form of copper carbonate. It is a mass of concretions made up of concentric veins of green in every shade and intensity. The most familiar variation is a rather deep blue-green variety that displays what appears to be an azure blue base.

Showing my students (and, even more so, large groups) how easily such complex images can be created usually evokes reactions of surprise if not bewilderment. There is more than one way to create such textures. Some artists will actually paint each positive concentric line onto the background. Others will use a negative technique in which they remove concentric lines with the tip of a cotton swab. This is fine if you need or wish to create a primitive work. These may be called fantasy or folk-art finishes. Besides being time consuming, however, such methods look contrived and artificial. That is not what faux finishes should be. They should, even if done in haste, be reasonable facsimiles of the real thing.

Since malachite is a semiprecious stone, this faux finish should be used with some discretion. In other words, don't paint an entire living room as if the walls are made entirely of this stone. Be reasonable and logical. Use it as an accent, in bands and in ornamentation. Let it remain believable. It helps the whole faux effect.

Besides being used to make jewelry, malachite is used in massive, polished form for ornamental purposes. It is also used for industrial application: When pulverized, it is a paint pigment. Artists usually grade

Materials

- cardboard (from frozen food packaging)
- Mediterranean blue-green satin or eggshell base
- glazing medium
- Phthalo Green, Raw Sienna and Raw Umber paints
- burler or short, round, white bristle fabric brush
- varnish or sealer

such pigments as organic, "real," organic emerald or smaragd green. Small samples of the stone may be purchased in many rock or souvenir shops for three to five dollars. However, you may have to tolerate getting an unfortunate magnet or key chain in the bargain. Better rock shops will have samples without these accessories and occasionally have nice, larger samples for perhaps thirty to sixty-five dollars.

Malachite

1 One of several techniques used to imitate malachite and similar agate effects employs pieces of cardboard. This method is not only among the most realistic, but also perhaps the easiest and quickest to execute. The cardboard used to package your favorite frozen food works best. Fold the cardboard, crease it very sharply, and fold it back and forth several times to enable you to tear it clean and straight. Do not bend the cardboard or depress the texture of the torn edges. These slightly frayed edges help you create the malachite images. Each edge is used only once because each will give you a different texture. The sizes should vary from about 1½ to 3 inches wide.

2 Mix a color of about five parts Phthalo Green and one part each of Raw Sienna and Raw Umber. Add glazing medium and apply it over a section of a Mediterranean blue-green satin or eggshell base coat. Move the edge of a section of your torn cardboard in a scalloped motion through the glaze.

3 Extend the glazed area so you can work wet-into-wet, and extend the groupings of malachite images, reversing them from the center of the surface out. These images may be shell-like but less uniform, and rather lucid and flowing, each image appearing somewhat like a puffy cloud on the horizon.

4 Although many individual malachite images in the real world form complete circles, do not attempt to complete them in your imitation. Unless practiced, this may cause unsightly build-up lines at the completion of each movement of the cardboard.

5 Be sure to cover all straight start-up lines at the beginning and completion of a move with a malachite image.

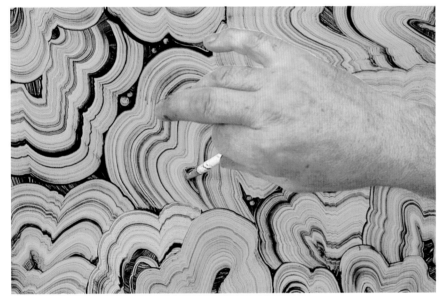

6 A well-executed piece of faux malachite requires strategy if not a little practice. Negative areas—those that display a pure dark green color—between individual malachite textures may display one or several very small malachite images. These are created, as in bur or burl wood imitations, with a burler or a short, round white bristle fabric brush.

7 The finished texture may be softened. This process requires some practice because of the edges built up by the displacement of glazes. (When the glaze is moved, some is removed and the rest is displaced. So when the cardboard is moved through the glaze, ridges are built up outside the edge of the cardboard.) Varnish or seal as needed.

Malachite (alternative colors)

1 Malachite can be any shade of green. The most common is similar to our previous sample. However, to enhance the overall appearance, you may need to blend in a secondary green glaze. This may be greener or include more Raw Sienna or Raw Umber, even a hint of Ultramarine Blue. As in the previous treatment, apply your glazes with separate brushes, and blend them well where they meet.

2 Work areas wet-into-wet, recognizing the short open time of acrylic paints and glazes.

3 Again, the finished product should be sealed or varnished. Refrain from even the most gentle and cautious sanding until adequate protection is applied.

Basket weave is a traditional nineteenth-century European technique that is occasionally found on wooden chair seats to imitate—yes, you guessed it—basket weaving. Even more interesting is that it is found as a background treatment in recessed panels of wardrobes.

This is an extremely easy technique, and that is where the problem lies. Rather than executing it one logical step at a time, we have the tendency to make things unnecessarily complicated by looking for shortcuts and trying to outsmart ourselves. Remember: Keep it simple.

The background color is often white, or one of a multitude of off-whites to assure adequate contrast between it and the glaze color. The latter is usually muted or earthy, like a dirty, so-called "institutional green," to name one example. The darker the glaze color is, the more the base can be tinted.

Again, contrast is important, as is a extremely thin, transparent glaze. Do not stop and think about it too much. Leave the painting surface straight and in front of you. In time, you will create a continuous flow of motion, which you may accompany with music. Strauss will do just splendidly!

Materials

- thin glaze in an earthy tone
- eggshell or satin base
- 1-inch (2.5cm) housepainting brush
- flat, sharp-chiseled bristle brush or heavy mottler brush

Basket Weave

1 A moderate coat of a very thin glaze is applied over a usually white or medium-colored eggshell or satin base. These effects appear best when the glaze color is somewhat "earthy" or "antique," or something with at least a hint of Raw Umber. Apply the glaze with a good-quality, 1-inch housepainting brush.

2 When the surface is coated, strié it with the brush in a 45° angle—this angle is corner to corner on a square (not a rectangular) surface.

3 Now using a clean, dry, flat, sharp-chiseled bristle brush—or even better, a heavy mottler brush—refine the strié effect by going over it.

4 This is your first weave. Now continue. Placing the bristle tips of the brush flat and straddling the corner, pull them against the grain of the first strié, 45° in the opposite direction.

5 Work the weave in a precise and orderly manner across the top edge of the surface. Be methodical, and always pull the weave all the way down at the proper angle, thus retaining disciplined movement and keeping the glaze open.

6 When the first row across is complete, reverse direction again. Work off the bottom edges of the previously created triangulars from the first weave. Complete the row.

7 Again reverse, working the weave in the opposite direction, and now working off of the bottom corner of the previously angled square. Remain controlled, calm and logical, proceeding step by step.

*I*t may be best to call this a fantasy or bravura finish because it is not a completely realistic imitation of travertine. It is, rather, a combination of the most easy-to-live-with elements of travertine and sandstone. In this case, the latter is a variety from Mankato in Minnesota. One client requested a treatment of this type of sandstone for his entry halls.

Sandstone is a sedimentary rock that is formed through the consolidation of sandbeds by pressure and binding materials. Sandstone colors are largely determined by the cementing material. Those bound by calcium, silica or clay are white, gray or pale yellow. Iron oxide gives the stone a red or reddish-brown color, and many mansions and building fronts have been built using these brownstones.

Mankato sandstone has a pleasant-looking surface with regard to its color and texture, but, to the faux finisher at least, it may be a bit boring. Many of the broken color techniques (fine stippling, mottling, sponging, frottage, wash, or a combination of these) would imitate the stone with at least reasonable success. Why bother, unless we can jazz up the texture a little bit?

Travertine is a crystalline rock formed by deposits of lime carbonate from fresh water in limestone or volcanic regions. Impurities may change the naturally white color of the rock to a great variety of different tints. When it is highly polished, the stone may resemble onyx. Many of the finest structures in ancient and modern Rome are built of this porous yet durable stone. It has also found wide application in turn-of-the-century and Art Deco theater lobbies and other public buildings in the United States.

Due to its concentric lines, which are more or less wavy, travertine is a wonderful stone to imitate. Since it is

Materials

- three different colors of glaze made from combinations of white, Raw Sienna, Burnt Sienna, Burnt Umber and Raw Umber
- several housepainting brushes
- cardboard (from frozen food packaging)

often used in construction, it can find equal use in our faux endeavors.

As mentioned earlier, travertine is porous—sometimes too porous. Dust and we-don't-want-to-know-what-else collects in these pea- to pebble-sized groups of pores. These details, realistic or not, are not necessarily something we need to live with. And so, with the power imbued to us as faux finishers, we may retreat into our own world and conveniently omit such inconvenient or ugly details.

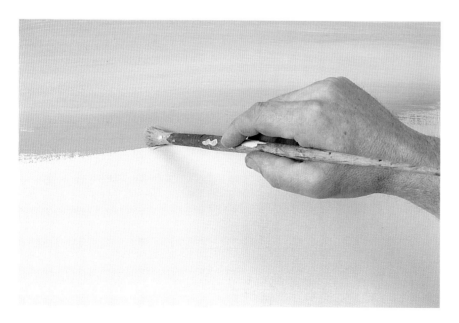

Travertine

1 This is a form of sandstone with a wide range of colors. This example is somewhat modified to resemble Mankato sandstone since most other travertine incorporates less dense, porous areas that often appear dirty, thus not always suitable for most people's home environment. Mix three separate colors out of combinations of white and Raw Sienna, Burnt Sienna, Burnt Umber and Raw Umber. Each color should be light but at least one to two shades darker than your sand-colored base. Make a rather transparent glaze of each color and apply them with separate brushes as blended bands onto the surface.

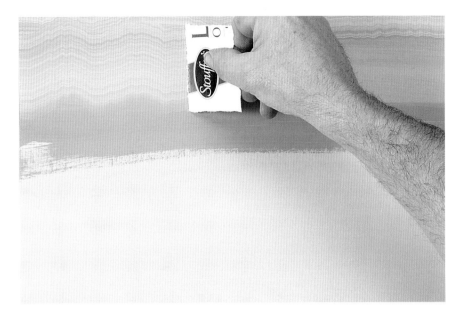

2 Cardboard, torn as in our malachite imitation, is employed very much like before. Here, however, instead of creating scalloped images, move the board in a comparatively straight direction, with some slight up-down movement through the glaze.

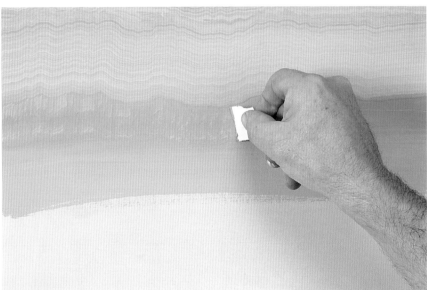

3 These movements should vary—some should be calmer, others more active. They should appear like different layers of sediment, so use different sizes of cardboard. They may be as wide as three to five inches. To create a better travertine effect as well as a more interesting texture, crosshatch the glaze below a band of fine line images. For this, the edge of your cardboard will work well.

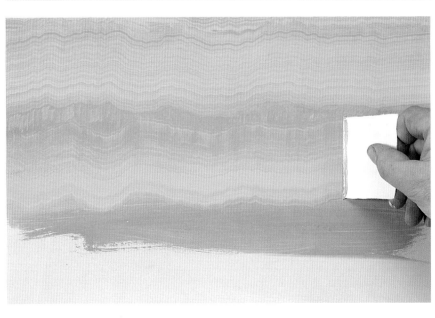

4 Extend the glazed area as required, blending the colored glazes where they meet. In some areas, the textures should be continuous. In other areas—for instance, where they were textured by hatching—they may open and close to create a more interesting overall look.

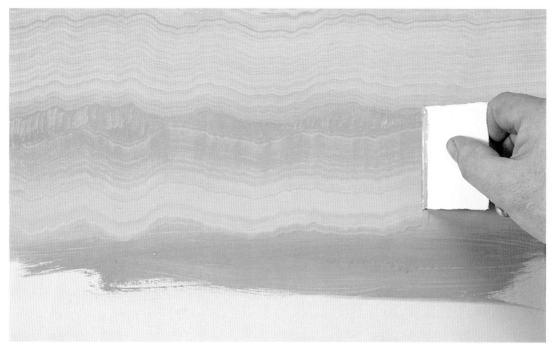

5 To create the appearance of a fracture, move the cardboard through the glazes. Stop and lift the cardboard off of the surface. Place it one-fourth to one inch higher and continue moving it through the glaze. This will make the lines appear offset, the sediments shifted.

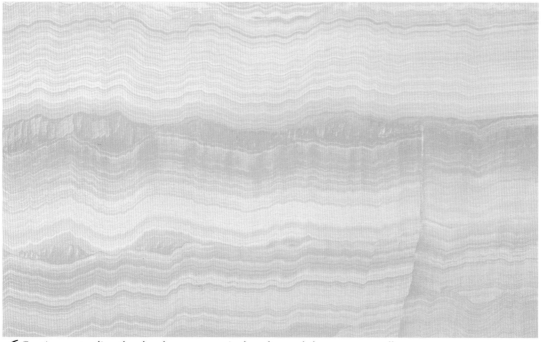

6 Continue extending the glazed areas as required, and extend the texture as well as any fractures you may have installed. Here, too, each move through the glaze must be executed with a new cardboard edge. The paper will absorb the liquid, causing it to become soft and without texture.

Travertine (demonstrating an effective layout)

1 One of the most common mistakes in wood and marble imitations is not so much questionable execution, but an ignorance of typical architectural considerations. No room is cut out of one single block of stone or a giant tree. In real life, spaces are built in manageable and logical sections or building blocks. The layout should conform to aesthetic and architectural standards as well as physical law to convey an impression of reality. Preparations for this may at times be demanding. Windows, doors and ornaments may prove a test of logic and mathematical skills rather than painting skills. Your ruler, pencil, levels, plumb line and calculator will prove to be valuable assistants.

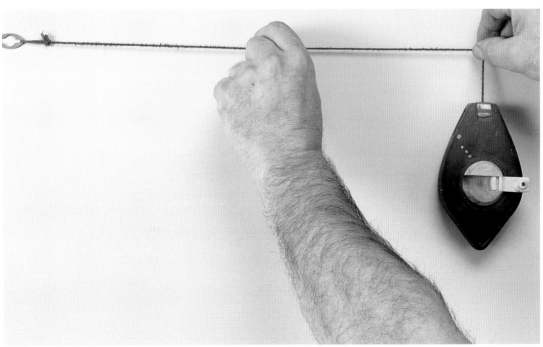

Materials

Layout

- ◆ ruler
- ◆ pencil
- ◆ level
- ◆ plumb line
- ◆ calculator
- ◆ ⅜-inch (1cm) masking tape
- ◆ malstock
- ◆ sable script liner brush
- ◆ flat-finish sealer or varnish

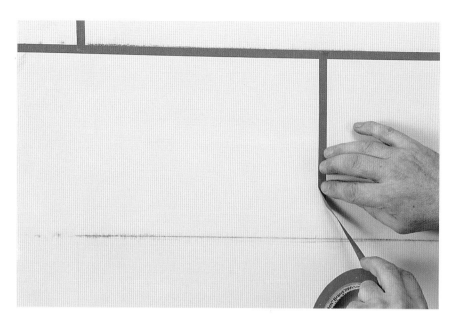

2 To create mortar joints, the use of tape is ideal. In this example, ⅜-inch tape was used to tape off the base color. This sand color will later become the light sides of the recessed grout lines.

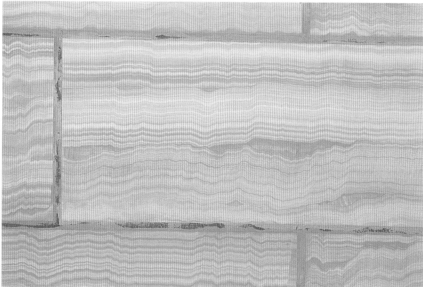

3 Marble the blocks as described earlier. Each block should be treated individually. The arrangement of the colors must vary, as should the width of the different bands of glaze and the structure of the textures.

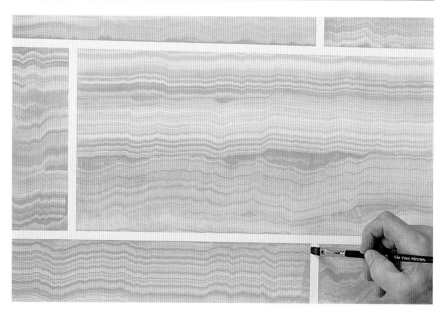

4 Remove the tape immediately behind your work and clean the miters (edges), paying special attention to those sides that are to remain light. If necessary, touch those up with the base paint.

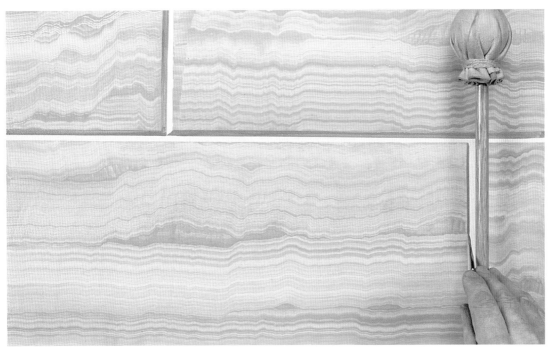

5 When the glazes are dry, add the shadows to the grout lines. Here a malstock (painting stick) and a sable script liner brush are used. These shadows should be placed according to the dominating natural light source. The color is not overstated. The addition of a small amount of Raw or Burnt Umber to your darkest glaze should be acceptable.

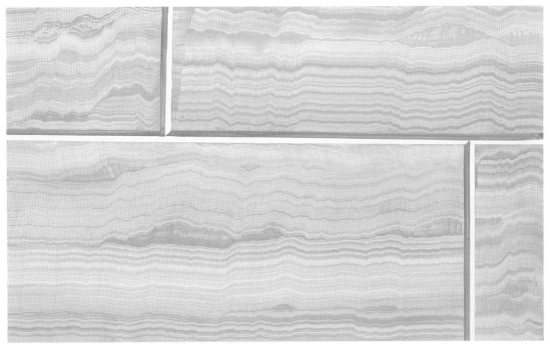

6 The finished product should appear as strong as a rock, yet delicate in texture and color. This makes it a pleasant, easy-to-live-with background. Since this finish imitates sandstone, a flat sealer or varnish is recommended.

**FINE ARTIST
AND FAUX FINISHING
BRUSHES AND TOOLS**

Faux Paw
4143 Hazel Street North
White Bear, MN 55110

The Faux Meister
148 Carpenter Street
P.O. Box 533
Dushore, PA 18614

**PAINTS, MEDIUMS
AND PIGMENTS**

Backstreet, Inc.
3905 Steve Reynolds Boulevard
Norcross, GA 30093

Catalina Cottage
125 North Aspan, #5
Azusa, CA 91702

Chroma, Inc.
205 Bucky Drive
Lititz, PA 17543

The Faux Meister
148 Carpenter Street
P.O. Box 533
Dushore, PA 18614

Polyvine
27825 Hopkins Avenue, #1
Valencia, CA 91321

WOOD SURFACES

Allen's Wood Crafts
3020 Dogwood Lane, Route 3
Sapulpa, OK 74066

Cabin Craft
P.O. Box 876
Bedford, TX 76095

Norse Enterprises
P.O. Box 307
St. Germain, WI 54558

Valhalla Designs
343 Twin Pines Drive
Glendale, OR 97442

QUALIFIED INSTRUCTORS

Karl-Heinz Meschbach & Friends
Atelier and School of
Fine Decorative Painting
148 Carpenter Street
P.O. Box 533
Dushore, PA 18614
Phone: (570) 928-8119
Fax: (570) 928-8290

Mike McNeil
330 SE Martin Luther King
Blvd.
Portland, OR 97214

Pro Faux
1367 Girard Street
Akron, OH 44301

ORGANIZATIONS:

*The National Society of Decorative
Painters*
398 North McLean Boulevard
Wichita, KS 67203
(393) 269-9300